A Treasury of Edith Hamilton

A TREASURY OF

EDITH HAMILTON

SELECTED BY

DORIS FIELDING REID

 W · W Norton & Company · Inc ·

NEW YORK

Frontispiece photo of Edith Hamilton by Roger W. Murphy.

FIRST EDITION

Copyright © 1969 by W. W. Norton & Company, Inc. All rights reserved. Published simultaneously in Canada by George J. McLeod Limited, Toronto. Library of Congress Catalog Card No. 70-90989. Printed in the United States of America.

SBN 393 04313 4

1 2 3 4 5 6 7 8 9 0

CONTENTS

INTRODUCTION

EDITH HAMILTON was born in the summer of 1867. Her home was in Fort Wayne, Indiana, where she was brought up surrounded by the Hamiltons: her grandparents, her parents, her uncle, her sisters, and her cousins. Her mother taught her French, their servants were all German, and she learned these two languages almost before she learned English. Her father started her on the classics at an incredibly early age. She wrote: "If a personal confession may be allowed, although I have read Latin ever since my father, who knew nothing about methods for softening the rigors of study, started me at the age of seven on 'Six Weeks' Preparation for Caesar', I have read it, except during the brief intermission of college, for my own pleasure merely, exactly as I would read French or German." At the advanced age of eight her father started her on Greek. The Greek language and ancient Greece then became a lifelong absorption. She did not go to school until she was sixteen years old, when she was sent to Miss Porter's School in Farmington, Connecticut. After that came Bryn Mawr College, where she won the European Fellowship and went to Germany to continue her studies in the classics.

In 1896 she became the first headmistress of the Bryn Mawr School in Baltimore, Maryland, where she remained until her retirement in 1922. Shortly thereafter she began her real career. Her first book, *The Greek Way*, was published in 1930. She died in 1963, and during the last some thirty-five years of her life she wrote seven books, introductions to the twenty-eight dialogues of Plato, and essays on a vast variety of subjects.

All of the books of Edith Hamilton are short and her writing is exceptionally condensed. "Why not just read her books?" was the nagging thought that kept coming to my mind as I began this volume.

I then realized that excerpts concentrating on a few of the major convictions that she expressed in all her books would be of interest to many readers. In quoting Edith Hamilton I have incorporated those writings which reflect the essence of her view of life in former times, and continue to influence our world today.

In these selections, all material translated from the Greek and Latin, unless otherwise attributed, is from Edith Hamilton's translations. The selections do not include quotations from one of Miss Hamilton's major works, *Mythology*. I found it was not possible to excerpt her important and illuminating introduction to this book. Nor have I included excerpts from her introductions to the *Collected Dialogues of*

Plato. These introductions seemed to me to be so interrelated that they would not be meaningful unless they were presented in their entirety.

One of Edith Hamilton's most deeply-felt convictions may not be immediately evident from these selections. In her preface to *The Roman Way*, she wrote:

"A people's literature is the great textbook for real knowledge of them. The writings of the day show the quality of the people as no historical reconstruction can. When we read Anthony Trollope or W. S. Gilbert we get an incomparably better view of what mid-Victorian England was like than any given by the historians. They will always be our best textbooks for an understanding of the force back of those years of unparalleled prosperity for the favored few. . . . That is the kind of textbook I have depended upon exclusively. For each period I have taken only the accounts given by contemporary writers."

The sources of the selections in this volume will be found at the end of the book.

DORIS FIELDING REID

December 1968

A Treasury of Edith Hamilton

MIND AND SPIRIT

GREECE AND THE
ANCIENT WORLD

FIVE HUNDRED YEARS before Christ in a little town on the far western border of the settled and civilized world, a strange new power was at work. Something had awakened in the minds and spirits of the men there which was so to influence the world that the slow passage of long time, of century upon century and the shattering changes they brought, would be powerless to wear away that deep impress. Athens had entered upon her brief and magnificent flowering of genius which so molded the world of mind and of spirit that our mind and spirit today are different. We think and feel differently because of what a little Greek town did during a century or two, twenty-four hundred years ago. What was then produced of art and of thought has never been surpassed and very rarely equalled, and the stamp of it is upon all the art and all the thought of the Western world. And yet this full stature of greatness came to pass at a time when the mighty civilizations of the ancient world had perished and the shadow of "effortless barbarism" was dark upon the earth. In that black and fierce world a little center of white-hot spiritual energy was at work. A new civilization had arisen in Athens, unlike all that had gone before.

. . .

Of all that the Greeks did only a very small part has come down to us and we have no means of knowing if we have their best. It would be strange if we had. In the convulsions of that world of long ago there was no law that guaranteed to art the survival of the fittest. But this little remnant preserved by the haphazard of chance shows the high-water mark reached in every region of thought and beauty the Greeks entered.

. . .

The causes responsible for this achievement, however, are not so generally understood. Rather is it the fashion nowadays to speak of the Greek miracle, to consider the radiant bloom of Greek genius as having no root in any soil that we can give an account of. The anthropologists are busy, indeed, and ready to transport us back into the savage forest where all human things, the Greek things, too, had their beginnings; but the seed never explains the flower. Between those strange rites they point us to through the dim vistas of faraway ages, and a Greek tragedy, there lies a gap they cannot help us over. The easy way out is to refuse to bridge it and dismiss the need to explain by calling the tragedy a miracle, but in truth the way across is not impassable; some reasons appear for the mental and spiritual activity which made those few years in Athens productive as no other age in history has been.

By universal consent the Greeks belong to the ancient world. Wherever the line is drawn by this or that historian between the old and the new the Greeks' unquestioned position is in the old. But they are in it as a matter of centuries only; they have not the hallmarks that give title to a place there. The ancient world, in so far as we can reconstruct it, bears everywhere the same stamp. In Egypt, in Crete, in Mesopotamia, wherever we can read bits of the story, we find the same conditions: a despot enthroned, whose whims and passions are the determining factor in the state; a wretched, subjugated populace; a great priestly organization to which is handed over the domain of the intellect. This is what we know as the Oriental state today. It has persisted down from the ancient world through thousands of years, never changing in any essential. Only in the last hundred years—less than that —it has shown a semblance of change, made a gesture of out- ward conformity with the demands of the modern world. But the spirit that informs it is the spirit of the East that never changes. It has remained the same through all the ages down from the antique world, forever aloof from all that is modern. This state and this spirit were alien to the Greeks. None of the great civilizations that preceded them and surrounded them served them as model. With them something completely new came into the world. They were the first Westerners; the spirit of the West, the modern spirit, is a Greek discovery and the place of the Greeks is in the modern world.

. . .

That which distinguishes the modern world from the ancient, and that which divides the West from the East, is the supremacy of mind in the affairs of men, and this came to birth in Greece and lived in Greece alone of all the ancient world. The Greeks were the first intellectualists. In a world where the irrational had played the chief role, they came forward as the protagonists of the mind.

. . .

Mind and spirit together make up that which separates us from the rest of the animal world, that which enables a man to know the truth and that which enables him to die for the truth. A hard and fast distinction between the two can hardly be made; both belong to the part of us which, in Platonic phraseology, draws us up from that which is ever dragging down or, in the figure Plato is fondest of, that which gives form to the formless. But yet they are distinct. When St. Paul in his great definition says that the things that are seen are temporal and the things that are not seen are eternal, he is defining the realm of the mind, the reason that works from the visible world, and the realm of the spirit that lives by the invisible.

In the ancient world before Greece the things that are not seen had become more and more the only things of great importance. The new power of mind that marked Greece arose in a world facing toward the way of the spirit. For a brief period in Greece East and West met; the bias toward the rational that was to distinguish the West, and the deep spiritual inheritance of the East, were united. The full effect of this meeting, the immense stimulus to creative activity given when clarity of mind is added to spiritual power, can be best realized by considering what had happened before Greece, what happens, that is, when there is great spiritual force with the mind held in abeyance. This is to be seen most clearly in Egypt where the records are fullest and far more is known than about any other nation of antiquity. It is materially to the point, therefore, to leave Greece for a moment and look at the country which had had the greatest civilization of all the ancient world.

In Egypt the center of interest was the dead. The ruling world-power, a splendid empire—and death a foremost pre-occupation. Countless numbers of human beings for countless numbers of centuries thought of death as that which was nearest and most familiar to them. It is an extraordinary circumstance which could be made credible by nothing less considerable than the immense mass of Egyptian art centered in the dead. To the Egyptian the enduring world of reality was not the one he walked in along the paths of everyday life but the one he should presently go to by the way of death.

There were two causes working in Egypt to bring about

this condition. The first was human misery. The state of the common man in the ancient world must have been wretched in the extreme. Those tremendous works that have survived through thousands of years were achieved at a cost in human suffering and death which was never conceived of as a cost in anything of value. Nothing so cheap as human life in Egypt and in Nineveh, as nothing more cheap in India and China today.

. . .

This instinctive recoil from the world of outside fact was enormously reinforced by the other great influence at work upon the side of death and against the use of the mind, the Egyptian priesthood.

Before Greece the domain of the intellect belonged to the priests. They were the intellectual class of Egypt. Their power was tremendous. Kings were subject to it. Great men must have built up that mighty organization, great minds, keen intellects, but what they learned of old truth and what they discovered of new truth was valued as it increased the prestige of the organization. And since Truth is a jealous mistress and will reveal herself not a whit to any but a disinterested seeker, as the power of the priesthood grew and any idea that tended to weaken it met with a cold reception, the priests must fairly soon have become sorry intellectualists, guardians only of what seekers of old had found, never using their own minds with freedom.

There was another result no less inevitable: all they

knew must be kept jealously within the organization. To
teach the people so that they would begin to think for themselves, would be to destroy the surest prop of their power. No
one except themselves must have knowledge, for to be ig-
norant is to be afraid, and in the dark mystery of the unknown a man cannot find his way alone. He must have guides
to speak to him with authority. Ignorance was the foundation
upon which the priest-power rested. In truth, the two, the
mystery and those who dealt in it, reinforced each other in
such sort that each appears both the cause and the effect of
the other. The power of the priest depended upon the darkness of the mystery; his effort must ever be directed toward
increasing it and opposing any attempt to throw light upon it.
The humble role played by the reason in the ancient world
was assigned by an authority there was no appeal against.

.   .   .

When Egypt ended, the East went on ever farther in the
direction Egypt had pointed. The miseries of Asia are a fear-
ful page of history. Her people found strength to endure by
denying any meaning and any importance to what they could
not escape. The Egyptian world where dead men walked and
slept and feasted was transmuted into what had always been
implicit in its symbolism, the world of the spirit. In India, for
centuries the leader of thought to the East, ages long since, the
world of the reason and the world of the spirit were divorced
and the universe handed over to the latter. Reality—that
which we have heard, which we have seen with our eyes and

our hands have handled, of the Word of life—was dismissed as a fiction that had no bearing upon the Word. All that was seen and heard and handled was vague and unsubstantial and forever passing, the shadow of a dream; only that was real which was of the spirit.

. . .

So the East found a way to endure the intolerable, and she pursued it undeviatingly through the centuries, following it to its farthest implications. In India the idea of truth became completely separated from outside fact; all outside was illusion; truth was an inner disposition. In such a world there is little scope for the observing reason or the seeing eye. Where all except the spirit is unreal, it is manifest folly to be concerned with an exterior that is less than a shadow.

As in Egypt, the priests saw their opportunity. The power of the Brahmans, the priestly caste, and of the great Buddhist hierarchy, is nothing less than stupendous. The circle is complete: a wretched populace with no hope save in the invisible, and a priesthood whose power is bound up with the belief in the unimportance of the visible so that they must forever strive to keep it an article of faith. The circle is complete in another sense as well: the wayfarer sheltering for the night in an abandoned house does not care to mend the roof the rain drips through, and a people living in such wretchedness that their one comfort is to deny the importance of the facts of earthly life, will not try to better them. India has gone the way of the things that are not seen until the things that are seen have become invisible.

That is what happens when one course is followed undeviatingly for ages. We are composite creatures, made up of soul and body, mind and spirit. When men's attention is fixed upon one to the disregard of the others, human beings result who are only partially developed, their eyes blinded to half of what life offers and the great world holds. But in that antique world of Egypt and the early Asiatic civilizations, that world where the pendulum was swinging ever farther and farther away from all fact, something completely new happened. The Greeks came into being and the world, as we know it, began.

. . .

The Greeks were the first people in the world to play, and they played on a great scale. All over Greece there were games, all sorts of games; athletic contests of every description: races—horse-, boat-, foot-, torch-races; contests in music, where one side outsung the other; in dancing—on greased skins sometimes to display a nice skill of foot and balance of body; games where men leaped in and out of flying chariots; games so many one grows weary with the list of them. They are embodied in the statues familiar to all, the disc thrower, the charioteer, the wrestling boys, the dancing flute players.

. . .

If we had no other knowledge of what the Greeks were like, if nothing were left of Greek art and literature, the fact that they were in love with play and played magnificently would be proof enough of how they lived and how they looked at life. Wretched people, toiling people, do not play. Nothing like the Greek games is conceivable in Egypt or Mesopotamia. The life of the Egyptian lies spread out in the mural paintings down to the minutest detail. If fun and sport had played any real part they would be there in some form for us to see. But the Egyptian did not play. "Solon, Solon, you Greeks are all children," said the Egyptian priest to the great Athenian. At any rate, children or not, they enjoyed themselves. They had physical vigor and high spirits and time, too, for fun. The witness of the games is conclusive. And when Greece died and her reading of the great enigma was buried with her statues, play, too, died out of the world. The brutal, bloody Roman games had nothing to do with the spirit of play. They were fathered by the Orient, not by Greece. Play died when Greece died and many and many a century passed before it was resurrected.

To rejoice in life, to find the world beautiful and delightful to live in, was a mark of the Greek spirit which distinguished it from all that had gone before. It is a vital distinction. The joy of life is written upon everything the Greeks left behind and they who leave it out of account fail to reckon with something that is of first importance in understanding how the Greek achievement came to pass in the world of antiquity.

. . .

A high-spirited people full of physical vigor do not obey easily, and indeed the strong air of the mountains has never been wholesome for despots. The absolute monarch-submissive slave theory of life flourishes best where there are no hills to give a rebel refuge and no mountain heights to summon a man to live dangerously. When history begins in Greece there is no trace of the ancient state. The awful, unapproachable sacred potentate, Pharoah of Egypt, priest-king of Mesopotamia, whose absolute power none had questioned for thousands of years, is nowhere in the scene. There is nothing that remotely resembles him in Greece. Something we know of the Age of the Tyrants in Greek history but what we know most clearly is that it was put a stop to. Abject submission to the power on the throne which had been the rule of life in the ancient world since kings began, and was to be the rule of life in Asia for centuries to come, was cast off by the Greeks so easily, so lightly, hardly more than an echo of the contest has come down to us.

.   .   .

Something completely new is here. The idea of freedom has been born. The conception of the entire unimportance of the individual to the state, which had persisted down from earliest tribal days and was universally accepted in all the ancient world, has given place in Greece to the conception of the liberty of the individual in a state which he defends of his own free will. That is a change not worked by high spirit and abounding vigor alone. Something more was at work in Greece. Men were thinking for themselves.

.   .   .

It is an extraordinary fact that by the time we have actual, documentary knowledge of the Greeks there is not a trace to be found of that domination over the mind by the priests which played such a decisive part in the ancient world.

· · ·

The sentences which Plato says were inscribed in the shrine at Delphi are singularly unlike those to be found in holy places outside of Greece. *Know thyself* was the first, and *Nothing in excess* the second, both marked by a total absence of the idiom of priestly formulas all the world over.

· · ·

In nearly every field of thought "they took the first indispensable steps." The statement means more than is apparent on the surface. The reason that antiquity did not give birth to science was not only because fact tended to grow more and more unreal and unimportant. There was an even more cogent cause: the ancient world was a place of fear. Magical forces ruled it and magic is absolutely terrifying because it is absolutely incalculable. The minds of those who might have been scientists had been held fast-bound in the prison of that terror. Nothing of all the Greeks did is more astonishing than their daring to look it in the face and use their minds about it.

· · ·

Love of reason and of life, delight in the use of the mind and the body, distinguished the Greek way. The Egyptian

way and the way of the East had led through suffering and
by the abnegation of the intellect to the supremacy of the
spirit. That goal the Greeks could never come within sight of.
Their own nature and the conditions of their life alike, shut
them off from it, but they knew the way of the spirit no less.
The all-sufficing proof that the world of the spirit was where
the flame of their genius burned highest is their art. Indeed
their intellectuality has been obscured to us precisely by vir-
tue of that transcendent achievement. Greece means Greek
art to us and that is a field in which the reason does not rule.
The extraordinary flowering of the human spirit which resulted in Greek art shows the spiritual power there was in
Greece. What marked the Greeks off from Egypt and India
was not an inferior degree of spirituality but a superior degree
of mentality. Great mind and great spirit combined in them.
The spiritual world was not to them another world from the
natural world. It was the same world as that known to the
mind. Beauty and rationality were both manifested in it. They
did not see the conclusions reached by the spirit and those
reached by the mind as opposed to each other. Reason and
feeling were not antagonistic. The truth of poetry and the
truth of science were both true.

. . .

Plato remarks in a discussion on how nations differ. "The
special characteristic of our part of the world is the love of
knowledge." "The Athenians," said St. Luke, "and the
strangers sojourning there spend their time in nothing else but
to tell or to hear some new thing." Even the foreigners caught

the flame. That intense desire to know, that burning curiosity about everything in the world—they could not come into daily contact with it and not be fired. Up and down the coast of Asia Minor St. Paul was mobbed and imprisoned and beaten. In Athens "they brought him unto the Areopagus, saying, 'May we know what this new teaching is?' "

. . .

There is a passage in Socrates' last talk with his friends before his death, which exemplifies with perfect fidelity that control of the feelings by the reason, and that balance between the spirit and the mind, which belonged to the Greek. It is the last hour of his life and his friends who have come to be with him to the end have turned the talk upon the immortality of the soul. In such a moment it would be natural to seek only for comfort and support and let calm judgment and cool reason loosen their hold. The Greek in Socrates could not do that. His words are:

At this moment I am sensible that I have not the temper of a seeker after knowledge; like the vulgar, I am only a partisan. For the partisan, when he is engaged in a dispute, cares nothing about the rights of the question, but is anxious only to convince his hearers. And the difference between him and me at the present moment is only this—that while he seeks to convince his hearers that what he says is true, I am seeking to convince myself; to convince my hearers is a secondary matter with me. And do but see how much I have to gain by this. For if what I say is true, then I do well to believe it; and if there be nothing after death, still, I shall save my friends from grief during the short time that is left me, and my ignorance will do me no harm. This is the state of mind in which I approach the argument. And I would ask you to be thinking of the truth and not of Socrates. Agree with me if I seem to you to speak the truth; or, if not, withstand me might and main that I may not deceive you as well as myself in my desire, and like the bee leave my sting in you before I die. And now let us proceed.

Thus in Greece the mind and the spirit met on equal terms.

.   .   .

The spirit has not essentially anything to do with what is outside of itself. It is mind that keeps hold of reality. The way of the spirit is by withdrawal from the world of objects to contemplation of the world within and there is no need of any correspondence between what goes on without and what goes on within. Not the mind but the spirit is its own place, and can make a Hell of Heaven, a Heaven of Hell. When the mind withdraws into itself and dispenses with facts it makes only chaos.

In the early days of the Restoration a great discussion was held by the learned men in the presence of the king on why, if a live fish were put into a brimming pail, the water would not overflow, while if the fish were dead, it would. Many elevating reasons that had to do with the inner significance of life and death were adduced for this spiritually suggestive property of water—or fish, until the king asked that two such pails be brought in and the fish added to them before his eyes. When it turned out that the water reacted in the same way to the fish alive or dead, the scientists received a lesson that had far-reaching results on the advisability of the mind's not going the way of the spirit and withdrawing into itself to exercise the pure reason free and unhampered, but of remaining strictly within the limits of the outside world. Abide by the facts, is the dictum of the mind; a sense for fact is its salient characteristic.

In proportion as the spirit predominates, this sense disappears. So in the Middle Ages when the West was turning more and more to the way of the spirit, the foremost intellects could employ their great powers in questioning how many angels could stand on a needle's point, and the like. Carry this attitude toward the world of fact a few steps farther and the result is the Buddhist devotee swaying before the altar and repeating *Amida* a thousand, thousand times until he loses all consciousness of altar, *Amida*, and himself as well. The activity of the mind has been lulled to rest and the spirit, absorbed, is seeking the truth within itself. "Let a man," say the Upanishads, the great Brahman document, "meditate on the syllable Om. This is the imperishable syllable and he who knowing this, loudly repeats that syllable, enters into it and becomes immortal." "God offers to everyone," says Emerson, "his choice between truth and repose. Take which you please —you can never have both." That is the West speaking and the way of the mind. Truth means, from this point of view, finding out about things—very active exercise.

· · ·

In Egypt, the reality of the unseen world slowly overshadowed that of the seen, but invisible though it was, it remained substantial. . . . The pyramids are as real as the hills. They look to be nothing made by hands but a part of the basic structure of the earth. Where the wind lifts the sand into shapes of a gigantic geometry—triangles which, as one watches, pass into curves and break again into sharp-pointed outlines, a cycle of endless change as fixed as the movement of the stars, against the immensity of the desert which never changes—the pyramids, immutable, immovable, are the spirit of the desert incased in granite. All the tremendous art of Egyptian sculpture has something of this unity with the physical world.

. . .

This hold on reality is something completely different from that grasped by the mind. It has nothing to do with the action of the mind; it is a profound intuition on the part of people whose consciousness has not yet divided them from the ways of nature. This intuitive feeling is as different from the conception of reality which the mind attains to as an Egyptian tomb, where life and death are hardly differentiated, is from that prison in which Socrates sat, trying to think out what was true in the hope of immortality.

. . .

The procedure laid down for a Buddhist artist before beginning his work is applicable in what it aims at to all Hindu art. He was to proceed to a place of solitude.

. . .

It is said of Polygnotus that when he wished to paint Helen of Troy, he went to Crotona, famed for the beauty of its women, and asked to see all those who were thought to be the most beautiful. . . .

The studio of the Greek was not a lonely cave of meditation, but the world of moving life. His picture was based on the women he had studied; it was conditioned by their actual bodily shapes; it was super-individual but not supernatural.

· · ·

A Brahman bronze of Shiva stands poised in the dance, arrested for a moment in an irresistible movement. Many arms and hands curving outward from his body add to the sense of and endless rhythmic motion. The shape, light, slim-waisted, is refined away from the human. Strange symbolic things surround him, deck him, a weaving cobra, a skull, a mermaid creature, long pendants waving from hair and ears, a writhing monster beneath his feet. His beauty is like nothing beautiful ever seen upon the earth.

The Olympic Hermes is a perfectly beautiful human being, no more, no less. Every detail of his body was shaped from a consummate knowledge of actual bodies. Nothing is added to mark his deity, no aureole around his head, no mystic staff, no hint that here is he who guides the soul to death. The significance of the statue to the Greek artist, the mark of the divinity, was its beauty, only that. His art had taken form within him as he walked the streets, watched the games, noted perpetually the people he lived among. To him what he saw in those human beings was enough for all his art;

he had never an impulse to fashion something different, something truer than this truth of nature. In his eyes the Word had become flesh; he made his image of the eternal what men could be. The Winged Victory is later Greek; the temple on the Acropolis was built to the Wingless Victory.

The endless struggle between the flesh and the spirit found an end in Greek art. The Greek artists were unaware of it. . . .

Athena was not a symbol of wisdom but an embodiment of it and her statues were beautiful grave women, whose seriousness might mark them as wise, but who were marked in no other way. The Apollo Belvedere is not a symbol of the sun, nor the Versailles Artemis of the moon.

. . .

The Greek temple is the creation, *par excellence*, of mind and spirit in equilibrium.

A few white columns dominate the lofty height at Sunion as securely as the great mass of the Parthenon dominates all the sweep of sea and land around Athens. To the Greek architect man was master of the world. His mind could understand its laws, his spirit could discover its beauty.

The Gothic cathedral was raised in awe and reverence to Almighty God, the expression of the aspiration of the lowly:

We praise thee, O God, we who are as nothing save in our power to praise thee.

The Parthenon was raised in triumph, to express the beauty and the power and the splendor of man:

Wonders are there many—none more wonderful than man.

Divinity was seen incarnate; through perfected mortality man was immortal.

. . .

The flowering of genius in Greece was due to the immense impetus given when clarity and power of thought was added to great spiritual force. . . . That union made the Athenians lovers of fact and of beauty; it enabled them to hold fast both to the things that are seen and to the things that are not seen, in all they have left behind for us, science, philosophy, religion, art.

. . .

The Greeks did not abstract away the outside world to prefer the claims of the world within; neither did they deny the spirit in favor of its incarnation. The things that are seen and the things that are not seen harmonized.

For a hundred years Athens was a city where the great spiritual forces that war in men's minds flowed along together in peace; law and freedom, truth and religion, beauty and goodness, the objective and the subjective—there was a truce to their eternal warfare, and the result was the balance and clarity, the harmony and completeness, the word Greek has come to stand for. They saw both sides of the paradox of truth, giving predominance to neither, and in all Greek art there is an absence of struggle, a reconciling power, something of calm and serenity, the world has yet to see again.

THE GREEK WAY
OF WRITING

THE ART OF THE Greek sculptors of the great age is known to us by long familiarity. . . . Our own sculptors learned their art from them, filled our galleries with reminiscences of them. Plaster casts more or less like them are our commonest form of inappropriate decoration. Our idea of a statue is a composite of Greek statues, and nothing speaks more for the vitality of the originals than their survival in spite of all we have done to them.

The same is true of the Greek temple. No architecture is more familiar to us. That pointed pediment supported by fluted columns—we are satiated with it. Endless replicas of it decorate the public buildings of all our cities and the sight of it anywhere is an assurance of something official within. Greece has been copied by sculptors and builders from the days of Rome on.

The art of the literature of Greece stands in singular contrast to these, isolated, apart. The thought of the Greeks has penetrated everywhere; their style, the way they write, has remained peculiar to them alone. In that one respect they have had no copyists and no followers. . . . English poetry has gone an altogether different way from the Greek, as has all the art that is not copied but is native to Europe.

This art, the art natural to us, has always been an art of rich detail. In a Gothic cathedral not an inch is left unelaborated in a thousand marvellous patterns of delicate tracery worked in the stone. In a great Renaissance portrait minutest distinctions of form and color are dwelt upon with loving care, frostwork of lace, patterned brocade, the finely wrought links of a chain, a jewelled ring, wreathed pearls in the hair, the sheen of silk and satin and furbordered velvet, beauty of detail both sumptuous and exquisite. It is eminently probable that if the temples and the statues of Greece had only just been discovered, we would look at them dismayed at the lack of any of the elaboration of beauty we are used to. To turn from St. Mark's or Chartres to the Parthenon for the first time, or from a Titian to the Venus of Milo never seen before, would undoubtedly be a chilling experience. The statue in her straight, plain folds, her hair caught back simply in a knot, no ornament of any description to set her off, placed beside the lady of the Renaissance or the European lady of any period, is a contrast so great, only our long familiarity with her enables us not to feel her too austere to enjoy. She shows us how unlike what the Greeks wanted in beauty was from what the world after them has wanted.

. . .

Greek writing depends no more on ornament than the Greek statue does. It is plain writing, direct, matter-of-fact. It often seems, when translated with any degree of literalness, bare, so unlike what we are used to as even to repel. All the scholars who have essayed translation have felt this difficulty and have tried to win an audience for what they loved and knew as so great by rewriting, not translating, when the Greek way seemed too different from the English. The most distinguished of them, Professor Gilbert Murray, has expressly stated this to be his method:

> I have often used a more elaborate diction than Euripides did because I found that, Greek being a very simple and austere language and English an ornate one, a direct translation produced an effect of baldness which was quite unlike the original.

The difficulty is there, no doubt, and yet if we are unable to get enjoyment from a direct translation, we shall never know what Greek writing is like, for the Greek and the English ways are so different, when the Greek is dressed in English fashion, it is no longer Greek.

. . .

Plain writing is not the English genius. English poetry is the Gothic cathedral, the Renaissance portrait. It is adorned by all that beautiful elaboration of detail can do. The words are like rich embroideries. Our poets may draw upon what they will to deck their poems. They are not held down to facts. Greek poets were. "The Greeks soar but keep their feet on the ground," said Landor. Our poets leave earth far behind them, freed by what the Greeks had small use and no name for, poetic license. Our minds are full of pictures of "caverns measureless to man, down to a sunless sea," of "flowers so sweet the sense faints picturing them," of "sermons in stones, books in the running brooks," of "magic casements opening on the foam of perilous seas," of "the floor of heaven thick inlaid with patines of bright gold . . . still quiring to the young ey'd cherubins." When Homer says, "The stars about the bright moon shine clear to see, for no wind stirs the air and all the mountain peaks appear and the high headlands," when Sophocles describes "White Colonus where the nightingale sings her clear note deep in green glades ivy-grown, sheltered alike from sunshine and from wind," when Euripides writes, "At high-tide the sea, they say, leaves a deep pool below the rockshelf; in that clear place where the women dip their water jars—" the words so literal, so grave, so unemphatic, hardly arrest our attention to see the beauty in them. Our imagery would have left the Greeks as cold. Clarity and simplicity of statement, the watchwords of the thinker, were the Greek poets' watchwords too. Never to them would the humblest flower that blows have brought thoughts that do often lie too deep for tears. A primrose by the river's brim was always a simple primrose and nothing more. That a skylark was like a glow-worm golden in a dell of dew or like a poet hidden in a light of thought, would have been straight nonsense to them. A skylark was just a skylark. Birds were birds and nothing else, but how beautiful a thing was a bird.

. . .

Everywhere fancy travels with a tight rein in the poetry of Greece, as everywhere in English poetry it is given free course. Byron uses no curb when he wants to describe a high mountain:

> —the monarch of mountains.
> They crowned him long ago
> On a throne of rocks, in a robe of clouds,
> With a diadem of snow.

When Æschylus has the same thing in mind, he will allow himself a single touch, but no more:

> the mighty summit, neighbor to the stars.

Coleridge is not using his eyes when he perceives Mont Blanc

> like some sweet beguiling melody,
> So sweet, we know not we are listening to it—

Pindar is observing Ætna with accurate care:

Frost-white Ætna, nurse all year long of the sharp-biting snow.

Coleridge was letting his fancy wander where it pleased. He was occupied with what he happened to feel when he stood before the mountain. Obviously he might have felt almost anything else; there is no logical connection between the spectacle and his reaction.

.   .   .

It follows that the fancy which must ever roam very far from home, played a humble role in Greek poetry. They never wanted to "splash at a ten-league canvas with brushes of comet's hair" [Kipling].

.   .   .

The influence of the English Bible has had its share in making the Greek way hard for us. The language and the style of it have become to us those appropriate to religious expression, and Greek religious poetry which makes up much of the lyrical part of the tragedies, perhaps the greatest of all Greek poetry, is completely un-Hebraic. Hebrew and Greek are poles apart. Hebrew poetry is directed to the emotions; it is designed to make the hearer feel, not think. Therefore it is a poetry based on reiteration. Everyone knows the emotional effect that repetition produces, from the tom-tom in the African forest to the rolling sound of "Dearly beloved brethren, the Scripture moveth us—to acknowledge and confess our manifold sins and wickedness; and that we should not dissemble nor cloak them—when we assemble and meet together—to ask those things which are requisite and necessary—" Nothing is gained for the idea by these repetitions; the words are synonyms; but the beat upon the ear dulls the critical reason and opens the way to gathering emotion. The method is basic in Hebrew poetry.

.   .   .

A familiar and completely characteristic example of the Hebrew way is the description of wisdom in Job:

But where shall wisdom be found? and where is the place of understanding? The depth saith, It is not in me: and the sea saith, It is not with me. It cannot be gotten for gold, neither shall silver be weighed for the price thereof. It cannot be valued with the gold of Ophir, with the precious onyx, or the sapphire. The gold and the crystal cannot equal it: and the exchange of it shall not be for jewels of fine gold. No mention shall be made of coral, or of pearls: for the price of wisdom is above rubies. The topaz of Ethiopia shall not equal it, neither shall it be valued with pure gold. Whence then cometh wisdom? and where is the place of understanding?—Behold, the fear of the Lord, that is wisdom; and to depart from evil is understanding.

The thought behind these sonorous sentences is simple: wisdom cannot be bought; it is the reward of righteousness. The effectiveness of the statement consists entirely in the repetition. The idea is repeated again and again with only slight variations in the imagery, and the cumulative effect is in the end great and impressive. It happens that a direct comparison with the Greek way is possible, for Æschylus too had his conception of the price of wisdom:

God, whose law it is that he who learns must suffer. And even in our sleep pain that cannot forget, falls drop by drop upon the heart, and in our own despite, against our will, comes wisdom to us by the awful grace of God.

. . .

We are lovers of beauty *with economy*, said Pericles. Words were to be used sparingly like everything else.

Thucydides gives in a single sentence the fate of those brilliant youths who, pledging the sea in wine from golden goblets, sailed away to conquer Sicily and slowly died in the quarries of Syracuse: "Having done what men could, they suffered what men must." One sentence only for their glory and their anguish. When Clytemnestra is told that her son is searching for her to kill her, all she says of all she feels, is: "I stand here on the height of misery."

Macbeth at the crisis of his fate strikes the authentic note of English poetry. He is neither brief nor simple:

> —all our yesterdays have lighted fools
> The way to dusty death. Out, out, brief candle!
> Life's but a walking shadow; a poor player
> That struts and frets his hour upon the stage—

The English poet puts before his audience the full tragedy as they would never see it but for him. He does it all for them in words so splendid, in images so poignant, they are lifted to a vision that completely transcends themselves. The Greek poet lifts one corner of the curtain only. A glimpse is given, but no more, but by it the mind is fired to see for itself what lies behind. The writer will do no more than suggest the way to go, but he does it in such a fashion that the imagination is quickened to create for itself. Pindar takes two lovers to the door of their chamber and dismisses them: "Secret are wise persuasion's keys unto love's sanctities." This is not Shakespeare's way with Romeo and Juliet. The English method is to fill the mind with beauty; the Greek method was to set the mind to work.

TRAGEDY AND COMEDY

TRAGEDY

TRAGEDY WAS A Greek creation because in Greece thought was free. Men were thinking more and more deeply about human life, and beginning to perceive more and more clearly that it was bound up with evil and that injustice was of the nature of things. And then, one day, this knowledge of something irremediably wrong in the world came to a poet with his poet's power to see beauty in the truth of human life, and the first tragedy was written. As the author of a most distinguished book on the subject says: "The spirit of inquiry meets the spirit of poetry and tragedy is born." Make it concrete: early Greece with her godlike heroes and hero-gods fighting far on the ringing plains of windy Troy; with her lyric world, where every common thing is touched with beauty—her twofold world of poetic creation. Then a new age dawns, not satisfied with beauty of song and story, an age that must try to know and to explain. And for the first time tragedy appears. A poet of surpassing magnitude, not content with the old sacred conventions, and of a soul great enough to bear new and intolerable truth—that is Æschylus, the first writer of tragedy.

Tragedy belongs to the poets. Only they have "trod the sunlit heights and from life's dissonance struck one clear chord." None but a poet can write a tragedy. For tragedy is nothing less than pain transmuted into exaltation by the alchemy of poetry, and if poetry is true knowledge and the great poets guides safe to follow, this transmutation has arresting implications.

Pain changed into, or, let us say, charged with, exaltation. It would seem that tragedy is a strange matter. There is indeed none stranger. A tragedy shows us pain and gives us pleasure thereby. The greater the suffering depicted, the more terrible the events, the more intense our pleasure. The most monstrous and appalling deeds life can show are those the tragedian chooses, and by the spectacle he thus offers us, we are moved to a very passion of enjoyment. There is food for wonder here, not to be passed over, as the superficial have done, by pointing out that the Romans made a holiday of a gladiator's slaughter, and that even today fierce instincts, savage survivals, stir in the most civilized. Grant all that, and we are not a step advanced on the way to explaining the mystery of tragic pleasure. It has no kinship with cruelty or the lust for blood.

On this point it is illuminating to consider our everyday use of the words tragedy and tragic. Pain, sorrow, disaster, are always spoken of as depressing, as dragging down—the dark abyss of pain, a crushing sorrow, an overwhelming disaster. But speak of tragedy and extraordinarily the metaphor changes. Lift us to tragic heights, we say, and never anything else. The depths of pathos but never of tragedy. Always the height of tragedy. A word is no light matter. Words have with truth been called fossil poetry, each, that is, a symbol of a creative thought. The whole philosophy of human nature is implicit in human speech. It is a matter to pause over, that the instinct of mankind has perceived a difference, not of degree but of kind, between tragic pain and all other pain. There is something in tragedy which marks it off from other disaster so sharply that in our common speech we bear witness to the difference.

All those whose attention has been caught by the strange contradiction of pleasure through pain agree with this instinctive witness, and some of the most brilliant minds the world has known have concerned themselves with it. Tragic pleasure, they tell us, is in a class by itself. "Pity and awe," Aristotle called it, "and a sense of emotion purged and purified thereby." "Reconciliation," said Hegel, which we may understand in the sense of life's temporary dissonance resolved into eternal harmony. "Acceptance," said Schopenhauer, the temper of mind that says, "Thy will be done." "The reaffirmation of the will to live in the face of death," said Nietzsche, "and the joy of its inexhaustibility when so reaffirmed."

Pity, awe, reconciliation, exaltation—there are the elements that make up tragic pleasure. No play is a tragedy that does not call them forth. So the philosophers say, all in agreement with the common judgment of mankind, that tragedy is something above and beyond the dissonance of pain. But what it is that causes a play to call forth these feelings, what is the essential element in a tragedy, Hegel alone seeks to define. In a notable passage he says that the only tragic subject is a spiritual struggle in which each side has a claim upon our sympathy. But, as his critics have pointed out, he would thus exclude the tragedy of the suffering of the innocent, and a definition which does not include the death of Cordelia or of Deianira cannot be taken as final.

The suffering of the innocent, indeed, can itself be so differently treated as to necessitate completely different categories. In one of the greatest tragedies, the *Prometheus* of Æschylus, the main actor is an innocent sufferer, but, beyond this purely formal connection, that passionate rebel, defying God and all the powers of the universe, has no relationship whatever to the lovely, loving Cordelia. An inclusive definition of tragedy must cover cases as diverse in circumstance and in the character of the protagonist as the whole range of life and letters can afford it. It must include such opposites as Antigone, the high-souled maiden who goes with open eyes to her death rather than leave her brother's body unburied, and Macbeth, the ambition-mad, the murderer of his king and guest. These two plays, seemingly so totally unlike, call forth the same response. Tragic pleasure of the greatest intensity is caused by them both. They have something in common, but the philosophers do not tell us what it is. Their concern is with what a tragedy makes us feel, not with what makes a tragedy.

Only twice in literary history has there been a great period of tragedy, in the Athens of Pericles and Elizabethan England. What these two periods had in common, two thousand years and more apart in time, that they expressed themselves in the same fashion, may give us some hint of the nature of tragedy, for far from being periods of darkness and defeat, each was a time when life was seen exalted, a time of thrilling and unfathomable possibilities. They held their heads high, those men who conquered at Marathon and Salamis, and those who fought Spain and saw the Great Armada sink. The world was a place of wonder; mankind was beauteous; life was lived on the crest of the wave. More than all, the poignant joy of heroism had stirred men's hearts. Not stuff for tragedy, would you say? But on the crest of the wave one must feel either tragically or joyously; one cannot feel tamely. The temper of mind that sees tragedy in life has not for its opposite the temper that sees joy. The opposite pole to the tragic view of life is the sordid view. When humanity is seen as devoid of dignity and significance, trivial, mean, and sunk in dreary hopelessness, then the spirit of tragedy departs. "Sometime let gorgeous tragedy in sceptred pall come sweeping by." At the opposite pole stands Gorki with *The Lower Depths*.

Other poets may, the tragedian must, seek for the significance of life. An error strangely common is that this significance for tragic purposes depends, in some sort, upon outward circumstance, on

pomp and feast and revelry,
With mask, and antique pageantry—

Nothing of all that touches tragedy. The surface of life is comedy's concern; tragedy is indifferent to it. We do not, to be sure, go to Main Street or to Zenith for tragedy, but the reason has nothing to do with their dull familiarity. There is no reason inherent in the house itself why Babbitt's home in Zenith should not be the scene of a tragedy quite as well as the Castle of Elsinore. The only reason it is not is Babbitt himself. "That singular swing toward elevation" which Schopenhauer discerned in tragedy, does not take any of its impetus from outside things.

The dignity and the significance of human life—of these, and of these alone, tragedy will never let go. Without them there is no tragedy. To answer the question, what makes a tragedy, is to answer the question wherein lies the essential significance of life, what the dignity of humanity depends upon in the last analysis. Here the tragedians speak to us with no uncertain voice. The great tragedies themselves offer the solution to the problem they propound. It is by our power to suffer, above all, that we are of more value than the sparrows. Endow them with a greater or as great a potentiality of pain and our foremost place in the world would no longer be undisputed. Deep down, when we search out the reason for our conviction of the transcendent worth of each human being, we know that it is because of the possibility that each can suffer so terribly. What do outside trappings matter, Zenith or Elsinore? Tragedy's preoccupation is with suffering.

But, it is to be well noted, not with all suffering. There are degrees in our high estate of pain. It is not given to all to suffer alike. We differ in nothing more than in our power to feel. There are souls of little and of great degree, and upon that degree the dignity and significance of each life depend. There is no dignity like the dignity of a soul in agony.

Here I and sorrows sit;
Here is my throne, bid kings come bow to it.

Tragedy is enthroned, and to her realm those alone are admitted who belong to the only true aristocracy, that of all passionate souls. Tragedy's one essential is a soul that can feel greatly. Given such a one and any catastrophe may be tragic. But the earth may be removed and the mountains be carried into the midst of the sea, and if only the small and shallow are confounded, tragedy is absent.

One dark page of Roman history tells of a little seven-year-old girl, daughter of a man judged guilty of death and so herself condemned to die, and how she passed through the staring crowds sobbing and asking, "What had she done wrong! If they would tell her, she would never do it again"— and so on to the black prison and the executioner. That breaks the heart, but is not tragedy, it is pathos. No heights are there for the soul to mount to, but only the dark depths where there are tears for things. Undeserved suffering is not in itself tragic. Death is not tragic in itself, not the death of the beautiful and the young, the lovely and beloved. Death felt and suffered as Macbeth feels and suffers is tragic. Death felt as Lear feels Cordelia's death is tragic. Ophelia's death is not a tragedy. She being what she is, it could be so only if Hamlet's and Laertes' grief were tragic grief. The conflicting claims of the law of God and the law of man are not what make the tragedy of the *Antigone*. It is Antigone herself, so great, so tortured. Hamlet's hesitation to kill his uncle is not tragic. The tragedy is his power to feel. Change all the circumstances of the drama and Hamlet in the grip of any calamity would be tragic, just as Polonius would never be, however awful the catastrophe. The suffering of a soul that can suffer greatly—that and only that, is tragedy.

It follows, then, that tragedy has nothing to do with the distinction between Realism and Romanticism. The contrary has always been maintained. The Greeks went to the myths for their subjects, we are told, to insure remoteness from real life which does not admit of high tragedy. "Realism is the ruin of tragedy," says the latest writer on the subject. It is not true. If indeed Realism were conceived of as dealing only with the usual, tragedy would be ruled out, for the soul capable of a great passion is not usual. But if nothing human is alien to Realism, then tragedy is of her domain, for the unusual is as real as the usual. When the Moscow Art Players presented the *Brothers Karamazoff* there was seen on the stage an absurd little man in dirty clothes who waved his arms about and shuffled and sobbed, the farthest possible remove from the traditional figures of tragedy, and yet tragedy was there in his person, stripped of her gorgeous pall, but sceptered truly, speaking the authentic voice of human agony in a struggle past the power of the human heart to bear. A drearier setting, a more typically realistic setting, it would be hard to find, but to see the play was to feel pity and awe before a man dignified by one thing only, made great by what he could suffer. Ibsen's plays are not tragedies. Whether Ibsen is a realist or not —the Realism of one generation is apt to be the Romanticism of the next—small souls are his dramatis personæ and his plays are dramas with an unhappy ending. The end of *Ghosts* leaves us with a sense of shuddering horror and cold anger against a society where such things can be, and these are not tragic feelings.

The greatest realistic works of fiction have been written by the French and the Russians. To read one of the great Frenchmen's books is to feel mingled despair and loathing for mankind, so base, so trivial and so wretched. But to read a great Russian novel is to have an altogether different experience. The baseness, the beast in us, the misery of life, are there as plain to see as in the French book, but what we are left with is not despair and not loathing, but a sense of pity and wonder before mankind that can so suffer. The Russian sees life in that way because the Russian genius is primarily poetical; the French genius is not. *Anna Karénina* is a tragedy; *Madame Bovary* is not. Realism and Romanticism, or comparative degrees of Realism, have nothing to do with the matter. It is a case of the small soul against the great soul and the power of a writer whose special endowment is *"voir clair dans ce qui est"* against the intuition of a poet.

If the Greeks had left no tragedies behind for us, the highest reach of their power would be unknown. The three poets who were able to sound the depths of human agony were able also to recognize and reveal it as tragedy. The mystery of evil, they said, curtains that of which "every man whose soul is not a clod hath visions." Pain could exalt and in tragedy for a moment men could have sight of a meaning beyond their grasp. "Yet had God not turned us in his hand and cast to earth our greatness," Euripides makes the old Trojan queen say in her extremity, "we would have passed away giving nothing to men. They would have found no theme for song in us nor made great poems from our sorrows."

Why is the death of the ordinary man a wretched, chilling thing which we turn from, while the death of the hero, always tragic, warms us with a sense of quickened life? Answer this question and the enigma of tragic pleasure is solved. "Never let me hear that brave blood has been shed in vain," said Sir Walter Scott; "it sends an imperious challenge down through all the generations." So the end of a tragedy challenges us. The great soul in pain and in death transforms pain and death. Through it we catch a glimpse of the Stoic Emperor's Dear City of God, of a deeper and more ultimate reality than that in which our lives are lived.

. . .

The literal translation of the first verse of the first choral song in *The Trojan Women* runs: "About Ilium sing to me, O Muse, with tears, an ode for the grave, of strange songs, for now I will loudly utter melody for Troy."

To my mind I am translating this faithfully when I write,

> Sing me, O Muse, a song for Troy,
> a strange song sung to tears,
> a music for the grave.
> O lips, sound forth a melody
> for Troy.

But of course Professor Murray thinks the same of his when he writes,

> O Muse, be near me now, and make
> A strange song for Ilium's sake,
> Till a tone of tears be about my ears
> And out of my lips a music break
> For Troy, Troy, and the end of the years.

And, presumably, the Loeb Classical Library people have the same opinion about their translator:

> O Song-goddess, chant in mine ear
>   The doom of mine Ilium: sing
> Thy strange notes broken with sob and tear
> That o'er sepulchres sigh where our dear dead lie:
> For now through my lips outwailing clear
>   Troy's ruin-dirge shall ring—

For myself, in my own translations I want to be accurate more than I want to be readable—although I recognize fully that if I make Æschylus and Euripides dull or ugly, I have done the most unpardonable thing a translator can do. Nevertheless I should not dare to add a thought of my own to these mighty masters in order to make it easier for the reader to understand them or to discover the beauty and the grandeur of what I can put so inadequately before him. If Euripides does not speak of sighing over sepulchers where the dear dead lie, then I will not.

. . .

Until the perfect, the final, translator comes, the plays should be perpetually retranslated for each generation. The present volume [*Three Greek Plays*] presents three of the greatest Greek tragedies translated into approximately the modern idiom. The two plays of Æschylus, *Prometheus* and *Agamemnon*, show best the range of his genius. The third play, *The Trojan Women* of Euripides, is the most modern in feeling of all Greek tragedies.

There are few efforts more conducive to humility than that of the translator trying to communicate an incommunicable beauty. Yet, unless we do try, something unique and never surpassed will cease to exist except in the libraries of a few inquisitive booklovers.

In this present enterprise, to give to three of the greatest of poetic dramas a temporary English life, the translator begs the help of the reader in recreating a past when tragedy was a purifying rite as well as a source of interest and emotion; a searching into the mystery of the universe as well as into the puzzle of the human heart. The obstacle of a different world added to that of a different language cannot be surmounted by the writer alone. "Piece out our imperfections with your thoughts."

．　．　．

It is hardly necessary to add that rhyme was not used by the Greek tragedians. To rhyme Æschylus is like rhyming Isaiah.

．　．　．

The great tragic artists of the world are four, and three of them are Greek. It is in tragedy that the pre-eminence of the Greeks can be seen most clearly. Except for Shakespeare, the great three, Æschylus, Sophocles, Euripides, stand alone.

．　．　．

Æschylus was the eldest of the three Greek tragic poets. He was the first writer of tragedy. Not the first, surely, to perceive it; where great souls suffer inexplicably, there tragedy is, never to be easily concealed or ignored. It has in it that which startles the mind to attention and brings the spirit up sharp against the enigma of human life. In all ages men must have discerned it and been baffled by it, but Æschylus was the first to write it. He conceived it so grandly and expressed it so adequately that there have been only three others fit to stand beside him, and those three, Sophocles, Euripides and Shakespeare, did their work after him, after he had put tragedy into literature.

．　．　．

The *Prometheus* is unlike any other ancient play. Only in the most modern theater is a parallel to be found. There is no action in it. Aristotle, first of critics, said that drama depends on action, not character. There is only character in the *Prometheus*. The protagonist is motionless, chained to a rock. None of the other personages do anything. The drama consists solely in the unfolding of Prometheus' character by means of conversation. It is the exemplar that tragedy is essentially the suffering of a great soul who suffers greatly.

.   .   .

Milton's Satan is often called Prometheus injected with Christian theology, but the comparison falls to the ground. For all Satan's magnificence, he is, to use Prometheus' words, "young—young." Shame before the other spirits keeps him from submission quite as much as his own ambition. Beside him Prometheus seems experienced. He has learned what is important to him and what is not. He is calmly strong, loftily indifferent, never to be shaken, because he is sure, both of what he wants and what he means to do. He stands forever as the type of the great rebel.

A more interesting parallel is with Job, who when wronged to the utmost submits to irresistible power. He knows that all Jehovah has done to him is utter injustice, but in the end, confronted with the Almighty who can divide the waters and find the way of the thunder and set bounds to the sea, Job gives up: "I know that thou canst do all things. . . .

Wherefore I abhor myself and repent in dust and ashes."
Prometheus, too, is faced by irresistible force. His body is
helplessly imprisoned, but his spirit is free. Just as with Job,
the unconditional surrender is demanded of him. He refuses.

To the herald of the gods who bids him yield to Zeus'
commands, he answers:

There is no torture and no cunning trick,
There is no force, which can compel my speech,
Until Zeus wills to loose these deadly bonds.
So let him hurl his blazing thunderbolt,
And with the white wings of the snow,
With lightning and with earthquake,
Confound the reeling world.
None of all this will bend my will.

HERALD

Submit, you fool. Submit. In agony learn wisdom.

PROMETHEUS

Seek to persuade the sea wave not to break. You will persuade me
no more easily.

HERALD

Remember well I warned you,
when you are swept away in utter ruin.
Blame then yourselves, not fate, nor ever say
that Zeus delivered you
to a hurt you had not thought to see.
With open eyes,
not suddenly, not secretly,
into the net of utter ruin
whence there is no escape,
you fall by your own folly.
(*Exit* HERALD.)

PROMETHEUS

An end to words. Deeds now.
The world is shaken.
The deep and secret way of thunder
is rent apart.
Fiery wreaths of lightning flash.
Whirlwinds toss the swirling dust.
The blasts of all the winds are battling in the air,
and sky and sea are one.
On me the tempest falls.
It does not make me tremble.
O holy Mother Earth, O air and sun,
behold me. I am wronged.

.   .   .

The *Agamemnon* holds the chief place among the seven plays of his [Æschylus] which have come down to us.

The play belongs to Clytemnestra, his heroine. Her only rival is the chorus into whose mouth Æschylus puts the greatest poetry he wrote. But Clytemnestra dominates the scene. Agamemnon, her husband, when he sailed for Troy ten years before, had sacrificed their daughter to the gods to get favorable winds for the fleet, and at that moment Clytemnestra made up her mind to kill him if ever he got back. The pathos and the horror of that sacrifice are vividly described; Æschylus intends us to realize what the girl's mother must have felt.

And all her prayers, cries of Father, Father,
her maiden life—
these they held as nothing.
Upon the ground

> fell her robe of saffron,
> and from her eyes
> sped an arrow
> that pierced with pity those that slew her.
> I see her there, a picture clear before my eyes.
> She strives to speak, as oftentimes,
> her father near, at the banquet table,
> she used to sing, the little maid,
> pure voice raised,
> honoring her father loved—

There was reason for Clytemnestra's implacable hatred. We are never allowed to forget her anguish of grief for her daughter, as well as her abhorrence of the father who killed his child. She speaks to the chorus of "What those dead suffered—that pain which never sleeps." It had never slept for her during all the ten years. It made her plan coolly and ruthlessly to murder her husband at the very moment of his triumphant homecoming.

She receives him upon his return with words of exultant joy that he has come back safe. She is exultant. Under their seeming falseness the words are true. His death before Troy would never have satisfied her. Her hand must strike him down. When he finally enters the palace where she will kill him, she pauses for a moment on the steps and prays, with what intensity,

> God, God, fulfillment is with thee. Fulfill my prayers.
> In thy care rests that which shall be fulfilled.

She is not a murderer in her own eyes; she is an executioner.

When the deed is done she comes out before the palace to proclaim it, but not defiantly. She is so justified to herself, she does not think of others. She has no idea of excusing herself until later the accusations of the chorus drive her to do so. She speaks with an overpowering rush of immense relief. Those ten years of desperate resolve are over.

> Long years ago I planned. Now it is done.
> Old hatred ended. It was slow in coming,
> but it came—

She is magnificent as she stands there, unshaken, speaking out all that she did and all that she felt, without a thought of concealment. His blood is on her face and dress and she is glad.

> So there he lay, and as he gasped, his blood spouted and splashed me with dark spray—a dew of death, sweet to me as heaven's sweet rain drops when the corn-land buds.

As Homer told the story, she killed Agamemnon because she had betrayed him with another man, but in Æschylus, even though she is the man's mistress and loves him, she kills her husband because he killed their daughter, for that reason only. When the chorus turns upon her and she must justify herself, her answer to them is,

> He cared no more than if a beast should die, when flocks are plenty in the fleecy fold, and slew his daughter, dearest anguish borne by me in travail—slew her for a charm against the Thracian winds.

Into that vengeance her lover did not come at all. She struck the blow, not he. The horrified chorus ask her,

> Who will make his grave?
> You? Will you dare who dared to kill him?

She answers, "Yes."

. . .

He [Æschylus] came to look at war in a way which was as unlike Marathon as possible and left it bare of glory.

> Women know whom they sent forth,
> but instead of the living,
> back there come to the house of each
> armor, dust from the burning.
> And War who trades
> men for gold,
> life for death,
> holding scales
> where the spear-points meet and clash—

It is strange that Æschylus came to think in that way. He did not watch Athens deteriorate during the war with Sparta, as Euripides did. He died long before, when the Periclean age was in its brilliant beginning, when thirty years of splendid achievement had followed after Marathon. And yet during those years he learned to see war as a business which sent men to die that other men might get rich.

. . .

No one ever felt the blackness of the evil always here with us more than he did, and no writing anywhere shows it blacker than the *Agamemnon* does. Nevertheless he did not in the end see it as senseless, signifying nothing. At the very least, he says, this is certain,

Knowledge won through suffering.
Drop, drop, in our sleep, upon our hearts,
sorrow falls, memory's pain,
and to us, though against our very will,
even in our own despite,
comes wisdom,
by the awful grace of God.

. . .

The greatest piece of anti-war literature there is in the world was written 2,350 years ago. This is a statement worth a thought or two. Nothing since, no description or denunciation of war's terrors and futilities, ranks with *The Trojan Women*, which was put upon the Athenian stage by Euripides in the year 416 B.C. In that faraway age a man saw with perfect clarity what war was, and wrote what he saw in a play of surpassing power.

. . .

He was the youngest of the three Greek tragic poets, but only a few years younger than Sophocles, who, indeed, survived him. The difference between the two men was great. Each had the keen discernment and the profound spiritual perception of the supreme artist. Each lived and suffered through the long-drawn-out war, which ended in the crushing defeat of Athens, and together they watched the human deterioration brought about during those years. But what they saw was not the same. Sophocles never dreamed of a world in which such things could not be. To him the way to be enabled to endure what was happening, the only way for a man to put life through no matter what happened, was to face facts unwaveringly and accept them, to perceive clearly and bear steadfastly the burden of the human lot, which is as it is and never will be different. To look at the world thus, with profundity, but in tranquillity of spirit, without bitterness, has been given to few, and to no other writer so completely as to Sophocles.

But Euripides saw clearest of all not what is, but what might be. So rebels are made. Great rebels all know the valley of vision. They see possibilities: this evil and that ended; human life transformed; people good and happy. "And there shall be neither sorrow nor crying, not any more pain: for the former things are passed away." The clarity with which they see brings them anguish; they have a passion of longing to make their vision a reality. They feel, like a personal experience, the giant agony of the world. Not many among the greatest stand higher than Euripides in this aristocracy of humanity.

Sophocles said, "Nothing is wrong which gods command." Euripides said, "If gods do evil, then they are not gods." Two different worlds are outlined in those two ideas.

· · ·

There is no plot in *The Trojan Women* and almost no action. After a ten-year war a town has been taken by storm and the men in it killed. Except for two subordinate parts the characters are all women. Their husbands are dead, their children taken from them, and they are waiting to be shipped off to slavery. They talk about what has happened and how they feel, and this talk makes up the substance of the play.

. . .

"Mother," the Trojan queen's daughter says, "I will show you,

> "This town, now, yes, Mother,
> is happier than the Greeks—
> They came here to the banks of the Scamander,
> and tens of thousands died. For what?
> No man had moved their land-marks
> or laid siege to their high-walled towns.
> But those whom war took never saw their children.
> No wife with gentle hand shrouded them for their
>   grave.
> They lie in a strange land. And in their homes
> are sorrows too, the very same.
> Lonely women who died. Old men who waited
> for sons that never came.
> This is the glorious victory they won.
> But we—we Trojans died to save our people.
> Oh, fly from war if you are wise. But if war comes,
> to die well is to win the victor's crown."

But many whom war kills cannot win that crown. The women talk little about the heroes, much about the helpless. They think of the children who are

> Crying, crying,
> calling to us with tears,
> Mother, I am all alone—

They see the capture of the city through their eyes; the terrible moment of the Greeks' entry as childish ears heard it:

> A shout rang out in the town,
> a cry of blood through the houses,
> and a frightened child caught his mother's skirt
> and hid himself in her cloak,
> while War came forth from his hiding place.

A child's death is the chief action in this play about war. A little boy, hardly grown beyond babyhood, is taken from his mother by the Greeks to be killed. She holds him in her arms and talks to him. She bids him:

> Go die, my best-loved, my own, my treasure,
> in cruel hands.
> Weeping, my little one? There, there,
> you cannot know. You little thing
> curled in my arms, how sweet the fragrance of you—
> Kiss me. Never again. Come closer, closer—
> Your mother who bore you—put your arms around
> her neck.
> Now kiss me, lips to lips—

When the little dead body is brought back, the mother is gone, hurried away to a Greek ship. Only the grandmother is there to receive it. She holds his hands,

> Dear hands, the same dear shape your father's had,
> how loosely now you fall. And dear proud lips
> forever closed.

She remembers the small boy climbing on to her bed in the morning and telling her what he would do when he was grown up.

> Not you, but I, old homeless, childless,
> must lay you in your grave, so young,
> so miserably dead.

"The poet of the world's grief," Euripides was called: in this play about war he sounded the deepest depths of that grief. How not, he would have said, since no other suffering approaches that which war inflicts.

COMEDY

"TRUE COMEDY," said Voltaire, "is the speaking picture of the Follies and Foibles of a Nation." He had Aristophanes in mind, and no better description could be given of the Old Comedy of Athens. To read Aristophanes is in some sort like reading an Athenian comic paper. All the life of Athens is there: the politics of the day and the politicians; the war party and the anti-war party; pacifism, votes for women, free trade, fiscal reform, complaining taxpayers, educational theories, the current religious and literary talk—everything, in short, that interested the average citizen. All was food for his mockery. He was the speaking picture of the follies and foibles of his day.

. . .

The playwright most like Aristophanes, the man whose sense of humor was most akin to his, lived in an age as unlike his as Shakespeare's was like it. The turbulent democracy that gave birth to the Old Comedy, and the England over whose manners and customs Queen Victoria ruled supreme, had little in common, and yet the mid-Victorian Gilbert of *Pinafore* fame saw eye to eye with Aristophanes as no other writer has done. The differences between Aristophanes and Gilbert are superficial; they are due to the differences of their time. In their essential genius they are alike.

The unknown is always magnificent. Aristophanes wears the halo of Greece, and is at the same time softly dimmed by the dust of centuries of scholarly elucidation. A comparison, therefore, with an author familiar and beloved and never really thought about wears a look of irreverence—also of ignorance. Dear nonsensical Gilbert, and the magnificent Aristophanes, poet, political reformer, social uplifter, philosophical thinker, with a dozen titles to immortality—how is it possible to compare them? The only basis for true comparison, Plato says, is the excellence that is peculiar to each thing. Was Aristophanes really a great lyric poet? Was he really bent on reforming politics or ending democracy? Such considerations are beside the point. Shakespeare's glory would not be enhanced if Hamlet's soliloquy was understood as a warning against suicide, or if it could be proved that in *Pericles* he was attacking the social evil. The peculiar excellence of comedy is its excellent fooling, and Aristophanes' claim to immortality is based upon one title only: he was a master maker of comedy, he could fool excellently. Here Gilbert stands side by side with him. He, too, could write the most admirable nonsense. There has never been better fooling than his, and a comparison with him carries nothing derogatory to the great Athenian.

Even in matters of technique, which is wont to vary so greatly from age to age, there are many similarities. To both men the fooling is the point, not the plot. In that subtle, individual thing, the use of meter, they are strikingly alike. The meter of a comic song is as important as its matter. No one understood that more clearly than Gilbert:

All children who are up in dates and floor you with 'em flat,
All persons who in shaking hands, shake hands with you like *that*.

Aristophanes understood it too as none better:

Come listen now to the good old days when the children,
    strange to tell,
Were seen not heard, led a simple life, in short were brought up
    well.

. . .

Politicians in Athens and in London seem very much the same. In the *Plutus* a slave, Carion, meets one. He asks:

    You're a good man, a patriot?
POLITICIAN: Oh, yes,
    If ever there was one.
CARION: And, as I guess,
    A farmer?
POLITICIAN: I? Lord save us. I'm not mad.
CARION: A merchant then?
POLITICIAN: Ah, sometimes I have had
    To take that trade up—as an alibi.
CARION: You've some profession surely.
POLITICIAN: No, not I.
CARION: How do you make a living?
POLITICIAN: Well, there're several
    Answers to that. I'm Supervisor General
    Of all things here, public and private too.
CARION: A great profession that. What did you do
    To qualify for it?
POLITICIAN: *I wanted it.*

So Gilbert in the song of the duke and duchess in the *Gondoliers:*

> To help unhappy commoners, and add to their enjoyment,
> Affords a man of noble rank congenial employment;
> Of our attempts we offer you examples illustrative:
> The work is light, and, I may add, it's most remunerative.
> Small titles and orders
> For Mayors and Recorders
> I get—and they're highly delighted.
> M. P.'s baronetted,
> Sham Colonels gazetted,
> And second-rate Aldermen knighted.

. . .

The woman joke, of course, is well to the fore with both men. It is ever with us. *Plus ça change, plus c'est la même chose.* Any number of passages might be selected.

The song of the duchess in the *Gondoliers* is completely in the customary style:

> On the day when I was wedded
>   To your admirable sire,
> I acknowledge that I dreaded
>   An explosion of his ire.
>
> I was always very wary,
>   For his fury was ecstatic—
> His refined vocabulary
>   Most unpleasantly emphatic.

Giving him the very best, and getting back the very worst—
That is how I tried to tame your great progenitor—at first!

. . .

Aristophanes' ladies are of quite the same kind. They form the chorus of the *Thesmophoriazusæ*, and they begin their address to the audience as follows:

We now come forward and appeal to you to hear how the men
    all flout us,
And the foolish abuse and the scandals let loose the silly things
    tell about us.
They say all evil proceeds from us, war, battles, and murder
    even;
We're a tiresome, troublesome, quarrelsome lot, disturbers of
    earth and of heaven.
Now, we ask you to put your minds on this: if we're really the
    plague of your lives,
Then tell us, please, why you're all so keen to get us to be your
    wives?

. . .

Parallels such as these could be given indefinitely. The world moves slowly. Aristophanes in Athens, fifth century, B.C., Gilbert in nineteenth-century England, saw the same things and saw the same humor in them. Some things, however, were seen by the Athenian which the Englishman was constrained not to see and this fact constitutes the chief point of difference between them. What a gulf divides the Old Comedy, so riotous and so Rabelaisian, and the decorous operettas that would never raise a blush on the cheek of Anthony Trollope's most ladylike heroine. A gulf indeed, but it is the gulf between the two periods. England's awful arbiter of morals, the formidable Queen in her prime, was the audience that counted in Gilbert's day, and it may be stated with

certainty that Aristophanes himself would have abjured indecency and obscenity in that presence. Equally certainly, if
he had lived in the age, *par excellence*, of gentility, he would
have tempered his vigor, checked his swiftness, moderated his
exuberance. Gilbert is an Aristophanes plentifully watered
down, a steady and stolid-y, jolly Bank-holiday, every-day
Aristophanes, a mid-Victorian Aristophanes.

The question is irresistibly suggested, if Gilbert had lived
in those free-thinking, free-acting, free-speaking days of
Athens, "so different from the homelife of our own dear
Queen," would he too have needed a Lord High Chamberlain

> To purge his native stage beyond a question
> Of "risky" situation and indelicate suggestion.

There are indications that point to the possibility, had he
not been held down by the laws the Victorian patrons of the
drama gave. He could not but submit to these limitations, and
only rarely, by a slip as it were, is a hint given of what he
might have done if there had not always been before him the
fear of that terrible pronunciamento: We are *not* amused!

But Aristophanes' audiences set no limits at all. Were
Plato's characters found among them, the meditative Phædrus,
the gentle-mannered Agathon, Socrates, the philosophic, himself? Beyond all question. They sat in the theater for hours on
end, applauding a kind of Billingsgate Falstaff at his worst
never approached; listening to violent invectives against the
men—and the women—of Athens as a drunken, greedy,
venal, vicious lot; laughing at jokes that would have put

Rabelais to the blush.

Such a theatre to our notions is not a place gentlemen of the Platonic stamp would frequent. A polite Molière comedy would be the kind of thing best suited to them, or if they must have improprieties to divert them, they should be suggested, not shouted. But our Athenians were not French seventeenth-century nobles, nor yet of Schnitzler's twentieth-century Vienna; they were vigorous, hardy, hearty men; lovers of good talk but talk with a body to it, and lovers quite as much of physical prowess; hard-headed men, too, who could drink all night and discuss matters for clear heads only; realists as well, who were not given to drawing a veil before any of life's facts. The body was of tremendous importance, acknowledged to be so, quite as much as the mind and the spirit.

Such were Plato's gentlemen and such were Aristophanes' audiences. The comic theater was a means of working off the exuberant energy of abounding vitality. There were no limitations to the subjects it could treat or the way of treating them. The result is that the distinctive quality of the Old Comedy cannot be illustrated by quotation. The most characteristic passages are unprintable. Something completely indecent is caricatured, wildly exaggerated, repeated in a dozen different ways, all fantastically absurd and all incredibly vulgar. The truth is that the jokes are often very funny. To read Aristophanes through at a sitting is to have Victorian guideposts laid low. He is so frank, so fearless, so completely without shame, one ends by feeling that indecency is just a part of life and a part with specially humorous possibilities. There is nothing of Peeping Tom anywhere, no sly whispering from behind a hand. The plainest and clearest words speak everything out unabashed. Life looks a coarse and vulgar thing, lived at the level of nature's primitive needs, but it never looks a foul and rotten thing. Degeneracy plays no part. It is the way of a virile world, of robust men who can roar with laughter at any kind of slapstick, decent or indecent, but chiefly the last.

. . .

Intellectuality and exquisite taste balanced by an immense vitality was the distinctive mark of the people—as Plato saw them.

But if ever a day comes when our intelligentsia is made up of our star football players we shall be on the way to understanding the Athenians—as Aristophanes saw them.

. . .

The traditional view is that Attic tragedy did not admit of comedy or humor. The textbooks all tell us that it was unrelieved by any lighter touch, and so gained an intensity of tragic effect impossible to Shakespeare's checkered stage of light and shade. But most readers will agree that the comedy of Ocean's talk with Prometheus is beyond dispute. Ocean is a humorous creation, an amiable, self-important old busybody, really distressed at Prometheus' hard fate, but bent upon reading him a good lecture now that he has him where he cannot run away; delighted to find himself the person of importance who has pull with Zeus and can get that unpractical fool, Prometheus, out of his not entirely undeserved punishment; but underneath this superior attitude very uneasy because of Zeus, who "isn't so far off but he might hear," and completely happy when Prometheus finally gives him a chance to save his face and run off safely home. When this dialogue is understood as humorous, the commentators and translators are relieved of what has always been a stumbling block to them, Ocean's four-footed bird. If it is accepted as axiomatic that a Greek tragic drama cannot have anything humorous in it, the bird with four feet undoubtedly presents difficulties. It is hard to see it as a tragic adjunct. But the Athenian spectators were at least as keen-witted as we are today, and when there appeared on the stage an enormous, grotesque bird with a pompous old man riding on its back, they had no more trouble than we should have in recognizing a comic interlude. Ocean is a figure of fun, and the steed he bestrides is there to give the audience the clue.

· · ·

Æschylus and Shakespeare alone stand for the soundness of Socrates' opinion, that it is within the province of the same writer to compose both tragedy and comedy. Lesser men would feel the intrusion of the comic into the tragic a fault against good taste, as witness all the critics who have suffered over the porter in *Macbeth*. But the great two, one surmises, were not concerned with good taste. They did what they pleased. A moment of tragic suspense, hardly to be equalled, is when the doors of Agamemnon's palace close upon the son who has come to kill his mother and has gained admission to her by pretending to be the bearer of the news of his own death. As he passes into the palace and the mind is full of the awful deed to be done, an old woman enters whom the chorus address as Orestes' nurse. She is crying:

Oh, I'm a wretched woman. I've known troubles enough but never any like this. Oh, Orestes, my darling! Oh, dear, he was the trouble of my life. His mother gave him to me to nurse, and the shrill screams at night that routed me out of bed, and all the useless bother of him. I had to put up with it. A child hasn't any sense, any more than a dumb beast. You've got to follow its whims. A baby can't tell you when it's hungry or thirsty or going to wet its clothes. And a child's stomach can do it all alone —and sometimes I knew what was coming, but often I didn't, and then all the clothes had to be washed. I wasn't only nurse, I was washerwoman too—

And so exits the forerunner of Juliet's nurse and the play moves on to the murder of the mother by her son.

. . .

When the curtain rings up for the stupendous drama which we know as Ancient Rome, it is raised surprisingly on two comic writers. They are the first to make their appearance on that mighty stage. The oldest piece of Roman literature we have is a collection of comedies. . . . Our notion of the proper beginning for the literature of the mistress of the world would be something martial and stirring. . . . But it

actually begins as far away from that as the wide realm of letters allows, in a series of comedies which are avowedly
founded upon the popular Greek comedy of the day.

. . .

There is no better indication of what the people of any
period are like than the plays they go to see. Popular drama
shows the public quality as nothing else can. But comedy does
more. It must present the audience, as tragedy need not, with
a picture of life lived as they know it. The comedy of each
age holds up a mirror to the people of that age, a mirror that
is unique. Ancient comedy, made up for us of four play-
wrights whose work alone has survived, the Greek Aristophanes and Menander, and the Roman Plautus and Terence,
is a mirror where may be seen vividly reflected the Greek and
Roman people in periods of notable significance to us.

. . .

Those who argue that they [Plautus and Terence] gave
their audiences not Rome but Greece, foreign folk whose
ways were strange to Romans, do not take into account the
nature of comedy. It must present the familiar. An easy understanding of what is going on is essential. Let puzzlement or
what follows inevitably in its train, disapproval, come in and
comedy is at an end. The audience are not there to have their
minds enlarged geographically or ethnologically. They want
to see people they know about and life lived in the way they

live it. A stray foreigner acting according to his own foolish foreign notions is a capital figure of fun, but a stage peopled with such would not be funny at all.

. . .

The people who laughed at these plays were on terms of friendly intimacy with their characters and found nothing "foreign" in their ways. Those who hold to the contrary might as well argue that Antipholus and Dromio, whose originals are in a play by Plautus, are Romans—or Greeks—and not Elizabethans. Shakespeare would never have attempted to people his plays with Romans. *The Comedy of Errors* has no more to do with Rome—or with Ephesus—than *A Midsummer-Night's Dream* has to do with Athens. The English stamp is upon the two Dromios just as clearly as upon Bottom and his crew.

. . .

Theories that go counter to the facts of human nature are foredoomed. Comedy in Rome to be comedy had of necessity to be Roman and no argument, linguistical, historiral, archæological, can have any counterbalancing weight against this fundamental truth.

. . .

The domestic drama, which is essentially the drama as we know it today, has its direct origin in these Latin plays [of Plautus and Terence]. The intimate domesticity of family life in one of its most impressive manifestations, the Roman family, is the pivot they all turn on, and character after character is shown which the theater has never let go of since. Here is the very first appearance upon the world's stage of the figure so dear to audiences everywhere, the Mother, essentially what she is to be through all the centuries down to our own with the white carnation and Mother's Day. Greece never knew her. The Mother, capitalized, was foreign to Greek ideas. But the Romans in such matters were just like ourselves and often more so.

. . .

The father has a place even more prominent. What they called in Rome the *Patria Potestas,* the Father's Authority, was clearly an awful matter.

But the authority of the master of the house had its limits. Plautus' Rome was the Rome of the Mother of the Gracchi and it is not difficult to understand that the Roman *Pater Familias,* weightily endowed though he was by law and edict and tradition, might meet his match in the determined virtues of the Roman matron. Indeed that resolute lady seems to be responsible for the creation of one of the most popular characters in literature, the henpecked husband. He makes his very first bow upon the stage in these plays.

. . .

A good-humored crowd, those people who filled the Roman theater in its first days of popularity, easily appealed to by any sentimental interest, eager to have the wicked punished—but not too severely—and the good live happily ever after. No occasions wanted for intellectual exertion, no wit or deft malice; fun such as could be passively enjoyed, broad with a flavor of obscenity. Most marked characteristic of all, a love of mediocrity, a complete satisfaction with the average. The people who applauded these plays wanted nothing bigger than their own small selves. They were democratic.

CLASSICISM AND ROMANTICISM

THE PECULIAR GIFT of the Greeks, to perceive the beauty of familiar, everyday things, and their art and literature which was concerned to reveal this beauty, is the great example of classic art and literature as distinguished from romantic. The Greeks were the classicists of antiquity and they are still to-day the pre-eminent classicists. What marked all they did, the classic stamp, is a direct simplicity in expressing the significance of actual life. It was there the Greek artists and poets found what they wanted. The unfamiliar and the extraordinary were on the whole repellent to them and they detested every form of exaggeration. Their desire was to express truthfully what lay at hand, which they saw as beautiful and full of meaning.

But that was not the Roman way. When not directly under Greek guidance the Roman did not perceive beauty in everyday matters, or indeed care to do so. Beauty was unimportant to him. Life in his eyes was a very serious and a very arduous business, and he had no time for what he would have thought of as a mere decoration of it.

. . .

Still, as Rome grew rich and strong and proud, she felt, of course, the need to display her power by a visible magnificence, and she built splendid temples and palaces and triumphal arches, but they were all Greekish—Greek seen through Roman eyes, bigger and better Greek. To the Roman the big was in itself admirable. The biggest temple in the world was as such better than the rest. If a Corinthian capital was lovely, two, one on top of the other, would be twice as lovely.

. . .

One of the great Victorians has said that if classicism is the love of the usual in beauty, romanticism is the love of the strange in beauty, and the statement gives to admiration the essence of the difference between the two. The very words romance, romantic, call up a vision, vague yet bright, that banishes the drabness and monotony of everyday life with a sense of possible excitements and adventures. Of course, if everyday life did not look drab and monotonous there would be no reason to turn to romance. That is primarily why the Greeks were not romantic. Facts were full of interest to them. They found enough beauty and delight in them to have no desire to go beyond.

But to the Romans facts were not beautiful nor, in themselves, interesting. The eagerness for inquiry into everything
in the universe which had stamped Greece never reached
Rome. Cicero's remark that the investigation of nature seeks
to find out either things which nobody can know or things
which nobody needs to know, expresses perfectly the Roman
attitude. . . . Their place was the world of practical affairs,
not of thought. Science ended as Greece went down and
Rome came up. Romans travelled all over the earth, but they
did not become geographers; they solved the problems of the
arch as it had never been done before, but they were not
physicists. They were persistently indifferent to theory. It
was enough for them to know that such a thing could be accomplished in such a way; the reason was unimportant. They
were not interested in why, only in how.

Beauty was still less interesting. It was never quite real to
them. Reality, facts, they saw as we do, chiefly as ugly and
unpleasant. "Face the facts," "Come down to reality"—the
phrases would have had the same meaning to the Romans that
they have to us. How hideous and grim reality can be was
forced upon their attention as it is not upon ours. We have
learned to protect ourselves by shutting away within stone
walls shocking sights, but in Rome after the great slave insur-
rection the main road to the city was lined for more than a
mile with the crosses of crucified slaves. Even the horrors of
war we disguise in part, but when a friend of Plutarch's vis-
ited a battlefield which had established an emperor on the
throne, he found bodies piled up sometimes as high as the

eaves of a little temple there. In plain, cold fact, reality, as they saw it was more often hateful than not. Their very amusements were perpetually showing them the horrible forms human agony and death can take.

When a people see chiefly ugliness in the world, they will find a refuge from it. Roman literature took the turn which literature has again and again taken when reality is perceived as nothing from which men can get spiritual delight. The writers of Rome's golden age of letters turned to romance.

.   .   .

To the classicist the nature of things is the truth and he desires only to see clearly what it is. The romanticist is the adventurer drawn on by the new and the strange where to him truth is to be found. The classic writer depends upon reason no less than upon imagination. To the romantic writer imagination can transcend the narrow limits of experience and move on unhampered by it to what eye hath not seen nor ear heard.

The *Æneid* from first to last is pure romance and Virgil, Rome's greatest poet, is one of the world's greatest romanticists.

.   .   .

Virgil and Livy inaugurated the new movement of the spirit the world was ready for. Classicism had grown thinner and dryer from the beginning of the fourth century B.C. on. It became precious, pedantic, all polished surface. Learning and style were the combination out of which to make poetry. This tendency is the evil genius of the classic spirit and has killed it many a time since the polite and erudite and cultivated society of Alexandria dealt it the blow which by the time Virgil appeared had been fatal to it.

． ． ．

To us romance means chiefly the passion of love. The Greeks, Plato excepted, did not think much of that as a subject for literature. They practically ignored it. Even Greek tragedy has very little to do with it. The romantic lover, we know, is allied to the lunatic, and the Greeks had a complete prepossession in favor of sanity.

． ． ．

Virgil could do a great love story. Æneas and Dido are not only the hero and heroine of our very first romance, they are great lovers, too, the woman the greater, as through the ages the poets have loved to portray her.

． ． ．

The episode of the hunting party [in the *Æneid*] is ushered in with all the trappings of romance. Before the palace door "Dido's charger splendid in purple and gold champs his foaming bit." The queen "comes forth with a great company attending her. Her cloak was purple bordered with embroidery; her quiver of gold, her hair knotted up with gold, her purple dress was fastened with a golden clasp." A hero's beauty in romance is quite as important as a heroine's, and when Æneas joins her he is "like Apollo as he leaves his wintry Lycia and visits Delos, his mother-isle; his flowing hair restrained by a wreath of soft leaves and entwined with gold; his arrows ring upon his shoulders. Even so swift came Æneas, such the beauty that shone forth from his peerless look and mien." Their union, when the hunt is broken up by the storm, takes place in surroundings perfectly fitted to two such personages, a Gustave Doré cavern lit by lightning flashes and echoing the roll of thunder and the cry of the mountain nymphs.

Virgil's attitude at this point in the story, the Roman attitude, was to have a far-reaching influence. Dido has made the fatal slip; her good name is lost; she has fallen from her high estate. Not so Æneas; the matter is merely incidental to him. His good name is not affected at all. . . . all that is left for Dido and her tarnished fair fame is death, the only refuge in such straits for the romantic heroine through all the centuries since.

Here is a great change from Homer and his treatment of Helen. A long way has been travelled on the long road of woman's destiny. In the *Iliad*, Helen is not blamed at all. What could a woman do but go with whatever man was at hand to carry her off? All the blame is put upon Paris. . . . But Roman women were not like that ever; they were responsible human beings, a force to be reckoned with; Dido clearly did not have to yield to Æneas. Then, by a curious shifting of the balance, all the blame was put upon her. Æneas got none of it. This was the Roman point of view, in line with all the early stories of Lucretia and Virginia and the like, and embodied in Virgil's poem it went over the whole Western world, never even challenged until almost the end of the nineteenth century. Trollope held it as firmly as Virgil. When lovely woman stooped to folly, her only refuge was to die, while the man in the case did just as Æneas did, married somebody else.

. . .

But just as there always follows close upon classicism the danger of . . . a pedantry that seeks only correctness and dispenses with life . . . so romanticism has an evil attending genius, sentimentality. The boundary between the two is so tenuous, so easily overpassed. Virgil transgressed it more than once. The romantic is imaginative, the sentimental is unreal; the romantic is idealistic, the sentimental is false. The mark of insincerity is upon all the sentimental: sentimentality is unconscious insincerity. The romanticist, as such, is as sincere as the classicist; it is only that his idea of truth is different. But the sentimentalist does not care about truth. He is always able to believe what he wants to believe.

. . .

They [the Athenians] were not tempted to evade facts. It is we ourselves who are the sentimentalists. We, to whom poetry, all art, is only a superficial decoration of life, make a refuge from a world that is too hard for us to face by sentimentalizing it. The Greeks looked straight at it. They were completely unsentimental. It was a Roman who said it was sweet to die for one's country. The Greeks never said it was sweet to die for anything. They had no vital lies.

. . .

Both trends, the classical and the romantic, have their dangers, which perpetually threaten to destroy them and often have destroyed them. The specter that haunts the classic artist is putting form ahead of spirit, style ahead of matter, polished convention ahead of free realism. The danger to the romantic, equally present whether he turns his back on ugliness or on loveliness, is sentimentality. It is easily recognized in the first case, but not in the second. There is a general impression that to describe things as dull and drab and unpleasant is realism and farthest removed from the roses and raptures of sentimentality. That is not true. The extremely unpleasant can be extremely sentimental. Sentimentality is always false sentiment. It is such a danger to the romantic artist because he has escaped from the domination of fact, and sentimentality is falsehood to fact. When an artist detests nature, he has thrown away his best defence against that danger. Nature is not sentimental. When Edgar Lee Masters describes a baby:

> She was some kind of a crying thing
> One takes in one's arms and all at once
> It slimes your face with its running nose,
> And voids its essence all over you,
> And there you stand smelling to heaven—

he has fallen into one extreme of sentimental unreality as truly as Swinburne has into the other when he writes:

> A baby's eyes—
> Their glance might cast out pain and sin,
> Their speech make dumb the wise,
> By mute glad god-head felt within
> A baby's eyes.

Neither Masters nor Swinburne, of course, were in the least concerned with what a baby is really like. They had escaped from that limitation. Perhaps each in his way was seeking for some other truth than the truth of nature, but all we know is that the result was falsehood for both of them, pure sentimentality, as much in the case of the nasty baby as in the case of the baby with the momentous eyes.

.   .   .

Forms of sentimentality vary in different ages and in different countries, but their common source is always easy to see. The Roman variety, of course, insisted upon human nature's being grand and heroic; dauntless courage and unshaken fortitude were the qualities all the sympathetic characters in their romance must possess.

.   .   .

All this is completely opposed to what the Greeks wanted. A Greek tragic drama had always, indeed, a romantic subject. The central idea of tragedy is rooted in strangeness, great souls suffering extraordinary calamities, but to the

Greek it must be presented classically, which is to say, in the way most opposed to the sentimental.

. . .

The idea of rewriting it [Greek tragedy] to suit modern Roman taste occurred to a very able man shortly after Virgil died and he became thereby the father of the sentimental drama.

His name was Seneca and he is best known as a statesman who for a few years held the reins in Rome, and as a devoted preacher of the Stoic doctrine. But his influence upon the theater is his most enduring title to fame.

. . .

Perhaps the most striking example of what resulted is his *Trojan Women*, based on Euripides' tragedy. A comparison between the two illustrates clearly the methods of the sentimental romantic.

In both plays the curtain rises upon the battlefield some days after Troy has fallen. Euripides shows an old woman asleep on the ground in front. As the day brightens she wakes slowly and lifts herself up painfully. She talks to herself in words that could be spoken only quietly, almost dully, as an old woman brought to the utmost of misery would speak:

> Who am I that I sit
> Here at a Greek king's door—
> A woman that hath no home,
> Weeping alone for her dead—

The whole speech is purely human; there is nothing in it of what we call a queenly spirit. To Seneca it seemed very poor, unworthy of royalty and sure to put a Roman audience completely off. His Hecuba is discovered erect with flashing eyes; her queenly spirit is visible in every inch of her, and her speech is delivered to the universe:

> Divinities, hostile to me and mine,
> I call you witness, and I call you too,
> Great sons, my children: bear me witness that
> I, Hecuba, saw all the woe to come.
> I saw it first nor did I fear to speak.
> I told you—

. . .

If literature is made up of the best, Seneca is unimportant for Latin literature, but the kind of drama he was the first to write has kept its popularity unimpaired down to today, and if great influence makes a great literary figure, he stands close to the first rank. In his plays the tendencies of Roman thought and feeling stand out in a form so heightened that they are unmistakable. He marks without the possibility of confusion the broad outlines of the Roman way as distinguished from the Greek way, and he is another proof that we are the inheritors not of Greece, but of Rome.

. . .

Our mechanical and industrial age is the only material achievement that can be compared with Rome's during the two thousand years in between. It is worth our while to perceive that the final reason for Rome's defeat was the failure of mind and spirit to rise to a new and great opportunity, to meet the challenge of new and great events. Material development outstripped human development; the Dark Ages took possession of Europe, and classical antiquity ended.

RELIGION

WHAT THE Greeks did for religion is in general not highly esteemed. Their achievement in that field is usually described as unimportant, without any real significance. It has even been called paltry and trivial. The reason people think of it in this way is that Greek religion has got confused with Greek mythology. The Greek gods are certainly Homer's Olympians, and the jovial company of the *Iliad* who sit at the banqueting board in Olympus making heaven shake with their shouts of inextinguishable laughter are not a religious gathering. Their morality, even, is more than questionable and also their dignity. They deceive each other; they are shifty and tricky in their dealings with mortals; they act sometimes like rebellious subjects and sometimes like naughty children and are kept in order only by Father Zeus' threats. In Homer's pages they are delightful reading, but not in the very least edifying.

If Homer is really the Greek Bible and these stories of his are accepted as the Greek idea of spiritual truth, the only possible conclusion is that in the enormously important sphere of religion the Greeks were naïve, not to say childish, and quite indifferent to ethical conduct. Because Homer is far and away the best known of the Greeks, this really is the prevailing idea, absurd as it must appear in face of the Greek achievement. There is no truth whatever in it. Religion in Greece shows one of the greatest of what Schopenhauer calls the "singular swing to elevation" in the history of the human spirit.

. . .

Greek religion was developed not by priests nor by prophets nor by saints nor by any set of men who were held to be removed from the ordinary run of life because of a superior degree of holiness; it was developed by poets and artists and philosophers, all of them people who instinctively leave thought and imagination free, and all of them, in Greece, men of practical affairs. The Greeks had no authoritative Sacred Book, no creed, no ten commandments, no dogmas. The very idea of orthodoxy was unknown to them. They had no theologians to draw up sacrosanct definitions of the eternal and infinite. They never tried to define it; only to express or suggest it. St. Paul was speaking as a Greek when he said the invisible must be understood by the visible. That is the basis of all great art, and in Greece great artists strove to make the visible express the invisible. They, not theologians, defined it for the Greeks. Phidias' statue of Zeus at Olympia was his definition of Zeus, the greatest ever achieved in terms of beauty. . . . "The Zeus of Phidias," said the Roman Quintilian, "has added to our conception of religion."

SOCRATES

"FOR THIS CAUSE came I into the world, that I should bear witness unto the truth." The words are in the Gospel of John, spoken by Christ to Pilate. Christ's witness to the truth was himself. He had no system of thought which could be considered apart from himself. It is clear that he took no care to pass on to future generations accurate statements of what he knew. He never wrote anything down.

. . .

Socrates too never tried to put the truth he had found into words. He thought as Christ did that it was impossible to tell men what it was and then expect them to know it. He too had no ordered philosophy or theology and he too never wrote a word down. Like Christ he lived his truth and died for it. A life can be more lasting than systems of thought. Socrates has outlasted two millenniums.

. . .

As a teacher of religion Socrates was a very odd figure, an evangelist such as there has never been before or since. . . . He never thundered anathemas as the men of righteousness have had the habit of doing against the wickedness of their times. Nothing could appear less like Isaiah and Jeremiah and all the other passionate reformers through the ages than he does as we see him in Plato's pages.

No one less dogmatic ever lived. He spent his life in the search for the truth; it was all-important to him, but he did not leave behind him one hard and fast definition. . . . "To find the Maker and Father of all is hard," he said, "and having found him it is impossible to utter him."

. . .

What he really was doing as he talked so easily and familiarly and humorously to the men of Athens, as he lived day by day so courteously and modestly and unobtrusively in his city that he loved, was establishing a new standard for the world. He believed with an unshakeable conviction that goodness and truth were the fundamental realities and that every human being had the capacity to attain to them. All men had within them a guide, a spark of the true light which could lead them to the full light of truth. This was Socrates' basic belief, in the words of the Gospel of John, "The true Light which lighteth every man that cometh into the world."

. . .

But it is not only or even chiefly through his faith in man and in God that he has lived for nearly two thousand five hundred years. It is because of what he himself was. He proved the truth of what he said by his life and even more by his death. He showed men what they could become, their own spiritual possibilities, and he showed them how they could meet "the mighty stranger, death." This great lesson was not obscured by later legends of marvels and miracles. No magical doings were ever related to Socrates.

. . .

The first effect he had upon his hearers was usually perplexity and bewilderment, sometimes it was extreme distress. Alcibiades, most brilliant in that brilliant town, told the company at the dinner table in the Symposium, "I have heard Pericles and other great orators, but they never troubled me or made me angry at living a life no more worth living than a slave's life. But this man has often brought me to such a pass that I could hardly endure to go on as I was, neglecting what my soul needs. I have sometimes wished that he was dead."

. . .

In prison a devoted friend, Crito, came to him, begging him, "O my beloved Socrates, let me entreat you to escape. Let us who can well afford it, bribe your way out of prison. Oh, be persuaded." Socrates answered serenely, "No. That cannot be. No one may do wrong intentionally. I will not break the law to save my life. I shall die, but I shall die innocent of wrong. This, dear Crito, is what a voice I seem to hear says to me and it prevents me from hearing any other. Yet speak, if you have something to say." "Socrates, I have nothing to say." "Then leave me, Crito, to fulfill the will of God and to follow whither he leads."

. . .

His intensity of conviction is what we are left with. Men can know what is true. And yet just before he died, in his last talk with his friends, for a moment he faltered. He was face to face with death. . . . What was he to meet after he drank the poison? Immortality or extinction? . . . That was what he faced and the darkness rolled over him as it did when Christ faced it upon the cross.

. . .

So Socrates loved the truth and so he made it live. He brought it down into the homes and hearts of men because he showed it to them in himself, the spirit of truth manifest in the only way that can be, in the flesh.

CHRIST

CHRISTIANITY IS Christ. "As the branch cannot bear fruit of itself, except it abide in the vine; no more can ye, except ye abide in me." To the degree that he is realized in each generation Christianity lives. To the degree that he seems unreal, remote, wrapped in a mist of strange words and incredible events, Christianity languishes.

Christ must be rediscovered perpetually. It is easy to read beautiful words of his and be moved by them, to accept him vaguely, not scrutinizing closely what has been recorded about him, preferring not to see him sharply in the clear air of truth. It is easy to keep him remote, put away in an atmosphere of unreality where his definite and practical demands to change the basis of human life can be dimmed into a kind of nebulous good will which exacts nothing in particular. But to study the records we have of him, to look at him closely and think out what he really meant, is dismaying because what he demanded Christians do not do and have almost never done. St. Matthew says, "It is enough for the disciple that he be as his master." Christ's disciples have not been as their master. The Christian life as we see it and live it is an easy life. All this and heaven too.

. . .

We must go back to Christ. The record of his life is light shining in the darkness to guide us. We must study it with simplicity, putting aside all that has come between us and it, religious conventions, incomprehensible statements, rituals, magical events. Back of all that mystification Christ stands. He can be found, but it is not easy; he has not only been hidden by trappings, he has been petrified, sanctified, deified, away from life. We have been taught to read the Gospels in a special way, not going to them to discover the facts about Christ, how he looked to the men who knew him, what he thought about life and death, the way he solved the problems all face. We use the Gospels as a manual of devotion, not a guidebook.

. . .

He is given to us drawn with a wonderful clarity, no blurred outline anywhere, carrying an overwhelming conviction of reality, so that never could he have been imagined; no one would ever have wanted to imagine him. He challenged men's dearest beliefs and most cherished institutions. He made demands that would have stripped the world bare of all it liked best.

. . .

When they [the Gospels] are read with serious attention, the kind of study one gives to something to be mastered, the result is startling. It is evident beyond a possibility of doubt that they contradict each other in a way no one could fail to see if he were not under the spell of familiar and venerated words. The evangelists differ when they are relating events as important as Christ's birth, death, resurrection, ascension, differences not trifling or subtle, but as striking as the disagreement about the place where Christ was last seen on earth, which one would suppose would have been ineradicably imprinted on the minds of those who there took leave of him; as important as the record of his last words on the cross, words most of all to be deeply treasured in the hearts of the hearers.

. . .

Christ is even represented as contradicting himself. Deeds and words are attributed to him which could not have been his except on the assumption that he said one thing at one time and the opposite at another, that he sometimes did what he later condemned. When there are such divergences and disagreements in the only record we have of him it might seem impossible to discover the real Christ, but the truth is that though the evangelists often differ about what he did and what he said, they never differ about what he was. That has been true through the ages. Extraordinarily, the bitter differences that divided Christians, the excommunications, the persecutions, the religious wars, were never due to different opinions about Christ himself. There people have always agreed. Christians fought each other to the death not on what he was, but on how he was to be explained. There are contradictions in the Gospels, but there is nothing contradictory in the person who emerges from them. He is the same, unmistakable in his individuality, unlike all others there have ever been. What is important is not that the record of him shows inconsistencies, but that he himself is always consistent.

· · ·

One thinks of the long line of those who, believing they were doing what would most please him, tortured themselves and others and made the test of being his follower the acceptance of a minute point in some bit of finespun theorizing. Which of them all was like him, who never held up suffering as a good, who said of himself that he "came eating and drinking," who declared that men would be judged not by their beliefs, but "Ye shall know them by their fruits," and whose own judgment was, "Neither do I condemn thee: go, and sin no more."

· · ·

Of all men anywhere, at any time, he [Socrates] came closest to the pattern Christ held up. His temper of mind was like Christ's. With an extraordinary elevation he combined a soberness and moderation very rare in the lives of the saints. In him as in Christ there was a complete absence of ecstasies and transports. . . . Christ said, "Seek and ye shall find." Find what? That he did not say. The conditions of finding he put into clear words. He that wills to do the will of God shall know. The only way to find the truth is to live it. The pure in heart shall see God. He said, "I am the truth." He was what he taught.

. . .

The Beatitudes are a series of assertions, unsupported, merely stated. Christ brought forward nothing to prove their truth; he pointed to no authorities; he used no argument. And those who heard him did not want any of those things, nor do we who read them. There is a realm of truth which stands by itself and is beyond argument. In an assertion there can be a finality which carries an instantaneous conviction that it is not open to question. No one has ever wanted to prove the Beatitudes.

. . .

Once when he had spoken briefly against confusing food with religion—the rules about preparing meat were many and minute—and had said that nothing that went into the mouth could defile a man, but only what came out of the mouth proceeding from the heart, his disciples told him in dismay that the Pharisees, especially given to ritual, "were offended when they heard this saying." The disciples' anxiety was natural. The Pharisees were the bulwark of learning and religion, and Christ had offended these revered teachers. Did he smile as he answered, "Let them alone, blind leaders of the blind"? With careless power he dismissed them. They were the intellectuals of his world, with a great tradition behind them. They did not matter to him at all, for he taught "as one having authority."

· · ·

The immense body of theological pronunciamentos does not find any support in his sayings. Ritual and ceremonial observances which are so easy and reassuring met with no mercy at his hands. The Sabbath is made for man, he said, not man for the Sabbath. That is one of his great freeing sentences, breaking through men's muddled values, making human welfare the only standard. But what did his hearers think to whom the sanctity of the Sabbath far outweighed any mere human good?

· · ·

Christ was even more explicit. He said at the last judgment men would be judged solely on the basis of how they had treated others. Not one word about their belief, only how they had acted to the unfortunate. . . . This was outrageous doctrine to men who had the fortifying consciousness of impeccably correct belief.

· · ·

When John and James came to him asking to sit on his right hand and his left "in thy glory," dazzling visions filling their young heads, Jesus said unto them, "Can ye drink of the cup that I drink of?" In the words there is something like a tender mockery of their childishness. They are not a genuine question; he knew the two could not know of what he was about to drink. They seem spoken as if he withdrew into himself to contemplate that cup which was then so very near. And he called the other disciples and said, "Ye know that they which are accounted to rule over the Gentiles exercise lordship over them, and their great ones exercise authority. But it shall not be so among you. . . . Whosoever of you will be the chiefest shall be servant of all." He valued not at all what we value.

· · ·

More and more he learned how alone he was. The crowds that came seeking him and listened to him, really wanted only marvels from him. "And he sighed deeply in his spirit and said, Why doth this generation seek after a sign? There shall no sign be given." "Yet learned he obedience by the things which he suffered," a verse in Hebrews says. "And being made perfect, he became the author of eternal salvation unto all them that obey him." There are a few indications of how he felt, his weariness and homesickness in "The foxes have holes and the birds of the air nests, but the Son of man hath not where to lay his head"; his question to the twelve when men were turning away from him, "Will ye also go away?" Most moving of all, as his certainty that he must die grew clearer, the longing to suffer it quickly and have it over: "I have a baptism to be baptized with, and how am I straitened till it be accomplished."

· · ·

He came to Jerusalem for the feast of the Passover and he was welcomed enthusiastically as "the King that cometh in the name of the Lord" by crowds who had not the least idea of a kingdom where the greatest was the servant of all. He was a wonder-worker to them who was somehow going to free them from paying taxes to the Romans. The priests looked deeper. They were powerful and prosperous and they did not want any change. Certainly they did not want Jerusalem to be a place where the last would be first and the first last. They were shrewd and conscientious too. This talk of setting men free, free even from the Sabbath, was highly dangerous.

. . .

With his arrest the crowds that had thronged around him melted away. His disciples all deserted him. Peter denied he had ever known him. No one was faithful to him, not even John whom he loved best. It was defeat, there could not be more complete defeat. There was not one in all the world to stand by him. The crowd—no doubt the same people who had cried to him a few days before, "Blessed is he who cometh in the name of the Lord"—were all shouting now, "Crucify him." No one ever was so alone. So they crucified him. "And he said, Father, forgive them, for they know not what they do." At that moment, as they nailed him to the cross and lifted it, his compassion for men was foremost, and his faith in them. The men who came to look at him said, "He saved others; himself he cannot save"—quite truly. His last hours on the cross were watched by his mother and a few friends. In St. Matthew's and St. Mark's record he spoke only once. Just before he died he cried, "My God, my God, why hast thou forsaken me."

Words which through all the centuries since have been a source of sorrowful wonder. No one ever denied that he said them. Never would anyone have wanted to make them up. They show as nothing else the fidelity of Christ's reporters. Terrible as they must have felt them, they wrote them down. Any effort to explain them is predestined to failure. Whoever understands them best shrinks most from enlarging upon them. One thing we know; if we set some radiant death, Stephen's perhaps, beside Christ's, we have a glimpse of something immeasurably greater and more profound in the agony of the cross than in the glory Stephen beheld as he died, and in some strange way Christ is closer to us. We read with awe those last words; they are beyond our grasp; and yet from the depths he reached he can touch all suffering mankind—because of the depths he reached. "Himself bore our infirmities." What would a serene death, a joyful death, a triumphant death, mean in comparison? In him the mystery of evil was shown at the moment of its greatest triumph; he died having failed, looking at the moment of death into blackness. And "behold, he liveth forever more."

FAITH

THE POWER OF Christianity, the power of all religion, is sustained by that strange capacity in us we call faith, a word very commonly used and very commonly misunderstood.

Ages of faith and of unbelief are always said to mark the course of history. The latter part of the nineteenth century with the emergence of modern science is the usual example of an age of unbelief. For the perfect example of an age of faith people have always been told, and are being told today with especial insistance, they must look back to mediaeval days. Of course it is beyond question that during the middle ages religion was very powerful, indeed supremely powerful; but there is a question whether the kind of religion that flourished then was such as to stamp the times as an age of faith. Certainly, the underlying motive which made many men profess religion had nothing to do with faith. It was fear, which is at the farthest remove from faith. There was a horrible place called hell, as actual as the earth itself, and once in it there was no escape to all eternity. Safety from that horror could be gained only by embracing religion. The idea was that of a perfectly sure and most profitable investment. Life was short, very short, indeed, during those centuries; immortality whether in heaven or hell very long; anyone could see the rationality of foregoing present brief advantage for an endless future profit. . . . It is evident that faith played no part here; it was a mere matter of common sense. Heaven and hell were substantial realities a man could invest in while here below, and no elaborate system of bookkeeping was needed to show which should be crossed out. The so-called Ages of Faith were only Ages of Certainty when men were sure they knew and understood all things in heaven as well as on the earth.

The church claimed to be the source of universal knowledge and her claim was allowed. She was possessed of indisputable information on every subject, not only heaven and hell and the roads that led thither, but the way the world came into being, how the heavenly bodies moved, what was the origin of man (and woman), why different languages arose, and so on, up to the exact constitution of the Holy Trinity. Nothing was as important as to accept these statements. Bliss or misery to all eternity depended upon doing so. How a man acted mattered not at all in comparison. The Inquisition burned people only for thinking incorrectly, not for living unethically.

. . .

Religion's chief function was to tell people what to think. It offered men that comforting possession, freedom from all personal responsibility. The mystery of human life was solved; no one need ever be disturbed by it.

It was a state of things which could last only as long as

men chose not to question it. . . . That is the reason religion had a great setback in the nineteenth century. The church had tied herself up to explanations which were outmoded. When the light of science was turned upon them and they were shown to be false, she and the cause of religion stood discredited. . . . The theologians had claimed the entire outside universe and they lost it. They had not an inch left in it to stand upon. Ideas for hundreds of years proclaimed as final truth were mere childishness in the new universe that was opening.

The church had arrogated to herself what did not belong to her. She had insisted that the reason which finds proofs and causes was her own province, and that the field of the mind which observes and organizes facts was indistinguishable from the field of faith. Then the mind and the reason turned against her and she suffered a great defeat.

. . .

When Christ said, "Blessed are they which have not seen, and yet have believed," he was describing faith. It belongs to that field of human activity which is concerned with making visible the things that are unseen. The field of faith has a common border with the field of art. That idea never dawned upon the great churchmen, but it would have been well for the church if it had.

During all the centuries of her life the church has made great use of art, but she has learned nothing from the artists. There was never an artist who did not know that he could not paint his picture or compose his music by thinking out the laws of beauty. . . . Science never had any quarrel with artistic truth, and the artists never concerned themselves with what the scientists said was true. The painters and the poets and the musicians know that there is an order of reality in which intellectual assurance plays no part and the reason is unimportant.

. . .

Faith is active. It has a driving power. It is vision which passes inevitably into action. "I have within me," said Euripides, "within my soul, a great temple of justice." That is the only place where justice is. Outside there is nothing but a dim distorted shadow of it. But its unreality in the world does not affect its reality to us nor the passionate protest of our heart when we see injustice. We know what justice is and that it is of first importance. It is real though all the facts say no. To know it thus as true, a truth one will never give up, an idea one will never abandon, is to be halfway on the road to faith in justice. Only halfway; faith is more than conviction. To have faith in justice is not only to perceive what justice is, how great and how excellent, it is also to be constrained to work for its realization, to try to make justice come to pass. Although it does not yet exist faith sees it, and acts to bring it into existence.

There is one definition of faith in the New Testament, only one, in the Epistle to the Hebrews. . . . "Now faith is the giving substance to things hoped for, the proving of things not seen."

. . .

THIS I BELIEVE

The following is the full text of a Radio Address written for the Series "This I Believe."

KEATS SAID, "I see in Shakespeare, the poet, the power of resting in uncertainty without any irritable reaching after fact and reason." What Shakespeare knew, he could not prove by fact and reason. In the truth he was seeking there could not be certainty, logically demonstrated or factually self-evident. There can never be that kind of certainty in the things that are greatest and most important to us. To me in the course of my long life, this has become a profound conviction. No facts, no reasoning, can prove to me that Beethoven's music is beautiful or that it is more blessed to give than to receive. No facts can prove to me that God is. There is an order of truth where we cannot have the proved certainties of the mind and where we do not need them. The search for spiritual truth may be hampered by them, not helped. When people are certain they know, the way to more knowledge is closed. But to perceive beauty opens the way to a fuller perception of beauty. To love goodness creates more goodness. Spiritual certainty leads to greater certainty.

The truths of the spirit are proved not by reasoning

about them or finding explanations of them, but only by acting upon them. Their life is dependent upon what we do about them. Mercy, gentleness, forgiveness, patience—if we do not show them, they will cease to be. Upon us depends the reality of God here on the earth today. "If we love one another God dwelleth in us." Lives are the proof of the reality of God.

When the world we are living in is storm-driven and the bad that happens and the worse that threatens press urgently upon us, there is a strong tendency to emphasize men's baseness or their impotent insignificance. Is this the way the world is to go or not? It depends upon us.

St. John spoke of the true light that lighted every man coming into the world. Belief in the indestructible power of that light makes it indestructible. This lifts up the life of every man to an overwhelming importance and dignity.

God leaves us free. We are free to choose Him or reject Him. No tremendous miracle will come down from heaven to compel us to accept as a fact a Being powerful enough to work it. What would that kind of belief do toward making love or compassion a reality? God puts the truth of Himself into our hands. We must carry the burden of the proof, for His truth can be proved in no other way. "Glorious is the venture," Socrates said.

EDUCATION

THIS EXTRAORDINARY CONQUEROR [Alexander the Great] had an extraordinary education. His father got for him the most remarkable tutor that ever tutored anyone. Aristotle taught him for a number of years. His father, Philip, king of Macedon, induced the great man to leave Greece and put Alexander in his hands when he was about thirteen. Plutarch tells us that he did not let them live with him but sent them off to a little town where they were practically alone together, an unschooled boy in his early teens and one of the greatest minds the world has ever known. Alexander's wonderful good fortune in this turn of events has been dwelt upon by practically everyone who has written about him, but clearly there is another side to the matter.

"The master of those who know" [Aristotle] had only one person to talk to. This was undoubtedly hard on him, but it was also hard on the thirteen-year-old boy. Aristotle was a scientist and a philosopher and a logician and a critic and an economist and a historian and an authority on ethics, and a master in every field he entered. Education too had engaged his attention. It was he who defined liberal subjects of study as opposed to utilitarian, and he had theories about the proper combination of the two. There is however no indication in what we know of him that when he was presented with Alexander he had ever had to put theory into practice, not even with the young considered as a class, much less with one definite young creature. Even that mighty mind must have felt unsure just at first until the habit of his life reasserted itself and he could go back comfortably to his own intellectual world. Inevitably one sees him pacing the road before the house—in Athens his custom was to walk while he lectured—talking about what was uppermost in his thoughts at the moment, with Alexander occasionally listening and wondering what it was all about, then diverted by some country sight or sound, then slipping away without the lecturer noticing that a small boy was missing.

Of all the subjects he listened to Alexander liked literature best. The historians gravely assure us that Aristotle's success as a teacher is proved by his pupil becoming a lover of Homer, but in those circumstances the *Iliad* must have seemed an oasis in the desert.

.   .   .

The fourth century [B.C. in Athens] was an age of great prose writers and of great school teachers. Poetry had distinguished the fifth century, which had had nothing much in the way of schools. In fourth-century Athens teachers were among the most famous men of the day. They founded their own schools, Plato the Academy, Aristotle the Lyceum, Isocrates, most popular of the three, a school of rhetoric, speech-making, Plato called it disdainfully. There were a number of others, too. Athens was full of educational fervor. Such times come for the most part when there is an increasing lack of confidence in the state. If people feel that things are going from bad to worse and look at the new generation to see if they can be trusted to take charge among such dangers, they invariably conclude that they cannot and that these irresponsible young people have not been trained properly. Then the cry goes up, "What is wrong with our education?" and many answers are always forthcoming.

· · ·

Aristotle did not found the Lyceum until some years after Plato's death, so that for the first half of the century there were only two great rival schools. The Academy's aim was to prepare men for philosophy with a dim and yet exciting possibility of producing or discovering among them a supremely good and great philosopher-ruler who would inaugurate the good state. Isocrates' school claimed to be a preparation for life and the purely intellectual was ruled out, except for mathematics, which he grudgingly conceded was good mental exercise, "a gymnastic of the mind" he called it. But that was his only concession in such ways. His school was practical, he said, designed to turn out young men fitted to play their part in the city's life.

Between Plato at the head of one theory of education and Isocrates at the head of the other, Athens had not an easy choice. Each school had ardent champions and the hot disputes were materially heightened by the two headmasters taking an active part in them. Isocrates attacked the very foundation of the Academy, declaring that Plato's idea of philosophy was fundamentally false. "Never," he said, "does that deserve the name of philosophy (the love of wisdom) which is of no immediate use." He was himself, he claimed, a true philosopher, clear-headed, realistic, sensible. "I hold that man wise who can usually think out the best course to take and that man a philosopher who seeks to gain that insight." A mere theorizer, he said, was incapable of it, a man of finespun speculations and lifeless abstractions.

He never mentioned his great rival by name, but here and there in his speeches, pamphlets rather, for although he taught oratory he was no orator and preferred writing to speaking, he dropped remarks about idealists who "busy themselves with impracticable plans" for the very practical matter of politics and "prefer to chatter empty nonsense rather than further some attainable good." He saw the relation of his thought to Plato's as that of the far-seeing statesman to the high-flying visionary. He was bent on a sweeping reform of political life which would result in bringing back the old personal independence and devotion to the state. Plato was bent upon the same thing, but to him the only way to benefit the state was for each Athenian to take a course which would benefit his own soul. One can see Isocrates' humorous shrug as he dismissed such foolishness.

Plato struck back and with harder blows. He held rhetoric in contempt and described the teachers of it as "Hunters after young men of wealth and position with sham education as their bait and a fee for their object." He dismissed as peremptorily their subject matter, Isocrates' "art of composing and delivering speeches" which he was so proud to teach. Plato says caustically in one of those comments of his which fling open a door and disclose a height not seen before, "Nothing spoken or written is of any great value if the object is merely to be believed, not to be criticized and thus learn more." The only writing that really brings profit is "engraving on men's souls justice and goodness and nobility." Sometimes he disguised his attack under an appearance of speaking jestingly, but the disguise was thin. He described "philosopher-politicians (a malicious phrase that hit Isocrates off to the life) who aim at being both and end by being neither." "But," he added kindly, "every man ought to be esteemed who pursues anything in the slightest degree like wisdom. Still, we shall do well to see them as they really are." It was a commendation nicely calculated to arouse Isocrates' fury.

· · ·

When Plato gave up politics and turned to teaching he was not in his own eyes withdrawing from the service of the state. To him that would have been a betrayal of the best. He says, "The greatest and fairest sort of wisdom by far is that which is concerned with the ordering of states." . . . To

find young men capable of leading and to develop to the full
their capacity by the right kind of education was now his object. The Academy might save Athens.

. . .

The Academy did not save Athens. It had a long life,
longer than any school there has ever been. . . . No great
and good leaders came from it, no philosopher-king to banish
injustice and establish good government on earth. We do not
know even of one who tried to do so.

. . .

It is our great loss that we know so little of what was
taught in the schools and how, but the most important matter
we do know, what their headmasters were like. We can conclude with security that there has never been a generation better educated than the one that ushered in the end of Athens.

. . .

We need the challenge of the way the Greeks were educated. They fixed their eyes on the individual. We contemplate the millions. What we have undertaken in this matter of
education has dawned upon us only lately. We are trying to
do what has never been attempted before, never in the history
of the world—educate all the young in a nation of over 170
millions; a magnificent idea, but we are beginning to realize
what are the problems and what may be the result of mass
production of education. So far, we do not seem appalled at

the prospect of exactly the same kind of education being applied to all the school children from the Atlantic to the Pacific, but there is an uneasiness in the air, a realization that the individual is growing less easy to find; an idea, perhaps, of what standardization might become when the units are not machines, but human beings. . . . Our millions spend hours before television sets looking at exactly the same thing at exactly the same time. For one reason or another we are more and more ignoring differences, if not trying to obliterate them. We seem headed toward a standardization of the mind, what Goethe called "the deadly commonplace that fetters us all."

. . .

The Bryn Mawr School in Baltimore, Maryland, was the first and only strictly college preparatory school for girls in the United States. In order to graduate, a girl was required to pass the Bryn Mawr College entrance examinations, and there was no alternative course. Edith Hamilton made the following comments about the curriculum.

The idea that we might be causing inferiority complexes never occured to me. The notion had not yet invaded school precincts and my own experience, far from leading me to it, made me convinced that the Bryn Mawr College entrance examinations could be passed by every girl who was willing to work hard, very hard in some cases, I admit.

But it is not hard work which is dreary; it is superficial work. That is always boring in the long run, and it has always

seemed strange to me that in our endless discussions about
education so little stress is ever laid on the pleasure of becoming an educated person, the enormous interest it adds to life.

The atmosphere of the school was not dull or depressing.
Again and again I saw that delightful thing, an awakening to
the joys of knowledge.

. . .

To be able to be caught up into the world of thought—
that is to be educated.

. . .

*The following comes from Edith Hamilton's unpublished
address at the seventy-fifth anniversary of the Bryn Mawr
School, October 1960.*

As I have looked back trying to think of memories to talk
to you about, one thing has come to me which I had never
quite realized before; how very hard it was for me to live up
to the school's sins! By that I mean I had to take them terribly
seriously, because the only punishment ever inflicted on any
of the girls was an interview with me; and very often they
were the kind of thing you just want to laugh over. . . . It
was up to me, even though my teachers were so good, to keep
the atmosphere of the school one where real life and book
learning were in the same world. It is so easy to get them
apart. I remember once, going into a classroom where a small
girl was beginning her recitation with "Achilles came out of
his tent on the seashore in front of a Greek camp and stood

looking over the main." It was so smooth I was suspicious. At last I said, "And what was the main, Emma?" She answered, "A ship blown up in the Spanish war." I got a very clear idea of how possible it was to learn words by heart without ever thinking of their making sense.

I can't say, though, that I myself ever thought much of college professors as educational guides for school girls. I know that is heresy, but I really think that. . . . I still remember with bitterness a Greek entrance examination where my girls, who had learned their Greek as Bryn Mawr College told them to, by reading Xenophon's *March of the 10,000* and *Iliad*'s battles of gods and men on the ringing plains of windy Troy, were asked to turn into Greek one of Aesop's fables about a frog! It was terrible and I still am angry when I think about it!

What I prized about the close connection of the school with the college was that it made hard work necessary. I can see myself sitting on the back stairs in the school building, telling a girl that she had failed her college entrance examination, and I can feel the heavy silence that got between us, and then I see her looking at me firmly and saying, "Well, I've got to put off making my debut at the Bachelors' Cotillion for a year." The Bryn Mawr School taught me that failure had its good side as well as its bad side. It did not need to create a complex; it could create courage. . . . Plato spoke for them all when he said with finality, "Hard is the good."

. . .

A wise and witty writer has said that the spirit of American education today is "if at first you don't succeed, try something else." That spirit has never invaded our school. There is a bit of Aristotle I always like to quote. He says it is a definition of happiness. It is that, but I think it also is what education should strive for: "the exercise of vital powers along lines of excellence, in a life affording them scope."

THE THING THAT HATH
BEEN IS THAT WHICH
SHALL BE

HOW OFTEN WHEN the dangerous youth of today are
being arraigned by despairing elders I have thought of Aristophanes or Xenophon or Isocrates yearning for "The good
old kind of education . . . when children were seen, not
heard." Now, all lament, the children are tyrants in their
families and hardly better in their schools. Alcibiades boxed
the ears of his literature teacher. What is the world coming
to? . . . That question is echoed by generation after generation . . . Cicero is credibly reported to have exclaimed, "O
tempora! O mores!" Never an age that is not appalled at its
own depravity.

. . .

There was a strong tradition of controlled art in a people
highly artistic by nature. It was thrown off by the generation

after the war apparently with complete ease. There is a new kind of music, Aristophanes says, which has driven out the old, and he declares that it is rubbish, a mixture of all kinds of incongruous melodies without rhythm or reason. The same is true of poetry. Poets are writing about whatever comes into their heads, "dolphins and spiders and prophets and race courses" all jumbled together with no regard for meter or for style. On the stage poetry had departed; only acting was important—and the applause of the crowd. This last was in point of fact supremely important; to capture it was the underlying motive of actor and musician and writer. Popularity was what they chiefly thought of as they tried novelty after novelty and one daring experiment followed another.

· · ·

The year was 431 B.C., when Athens was mistress of the sea, when Sparta had the best army in the world—and Persia saw a prospect of being rid of both at no more cost than encouraging first one and then the other.

The greatest sea power in Europe and the greatest land power faced each other in war. The stake was the leadership of Europe. Each was fighting to strengthen her own position at the expense of the other: in the case of the sea power to hold her widely separated empire; in the case of the land power to challenge that empire and win one for herself. Both, as the war began, were uneasily conscious that an important and even decisive factor might be an Asiatic nation, enormous in extent of territory, which had a foothold in Europe and was believed by many to be interested in watching the two chief Western powers weaken and perhaps destroy each other until in the end she herself could easily dominate Europe.

Historians today generally reject the idea that history repeats itself and may therefore be studied as a warning and a guide. The modern scientific historian looks at his subject very much as the geologist does. History is a chronicle of fact considered for itself alone. There is no pattern in the web unrolled from the loom of time and no profit in studying it except to gain information. That was not the point of view of the Greek historian of the war between Athens and Sparta, whose book is still a masterpiece among histories. . . . Thucydides wrote his book because he believed that men would profit from a knowledge of what brought about that ruinous struggle precisely as they profit from a statement of what causes a deadly disease. He reasoned that since the nature of the human mind does not change any more than the nature of the human body, circumstances swayed by human nature are bound to repeat themselves, and in the same situation men are bound to act in the same way unless it is shown to them that such a course in other days ended disastrously. When the reason why a disaster came about is perceived people will be able to guard against that particular danger. "It will perhaps be found," he writes, "that the absence of storytelling in my work makes it less attractive to listen to, but I shall be satisfied if it is considered useful by all who wish to know the plain truth of the events which happened and will according to human nature happen again in the same way. It was written not for the moment, but for all time."

. . .

All readers approach Thucydides with a preconception in favor of Athens. The Spartans have left the world nothing in the way of art or literature or science. Nevertheless it must be said that the Spartan ideal has remained persistent from their day to our own, the manifestation of an instinct hardly weakened through the last two thousand years. It is not an adult point of view. Sparta looked at things the way schoolboys do, very much like Kipling's Stalky & Co. The Ideal Spartan was plucky, indifferent to hardship and pain, a first-rate athlete. The less he talked or, for that matter, thought, the better. It was for him emphatically not to reason why, but always to do and die. He was a soldier and nothing else. The purpose of the Spartan state was war. The Athenians were realistic in their attitude toward war as toward everything else. They saw nothing attractive in dying on the battlefield. Pericles, in the oration Thucydides reports him as delivering over those who had fallen in battle, does not urge his hearers to go and do likewise, but bids them pray that if they fight it will be in less dangerous circumstances. War was a bad business in Athens. Nevertheless it was a necessity; the only way a state could take what belonged to others and, having taken, keep it. War could, of course, be very profitable.

. . .

The war had nothing to do with differences in ideas or with considerations of right and wrong. Is democracy right and the rule of the few over the many wrong? To Thucydides the question would have seemed an evasion of the issue. There was no right power. Power, whoever wielded it, was evil, the corruptor of men.

A historian who lived some two hundred years later, Polybius, also a Greek, gives an admirably clear and condensed account of Thucydides' basic thesis. Human history, he says, is a cycle which excess of power keeps revolving. Primitive despots start the wheel rolling. The more power they get the more they want, and they go on abusing their authority until inevitably opposition is aroused and a few men, strong enough when they unite, seize the rule for themselves. These, too, can never be satisfied. They encroach upon the rights of others until they are opposed in their turn. The people are aroused against them, and democracy succeeds to oligarchy. But there again the evil in all power is no less operative. It brings corruption and contempt for law, until the state can no longer function and falls easily before a strong man who promises to restore order. The rule of the one, of the few, of the many, each is destroyed in turn because there is in them all an unvarying evil—the greed for power—and no moral quality is necessarily bound up with any of them.

The revolution of the cycle Thucydides watched brought results so terrible that he believed an account of them would be a warning which men could not disregard.

. . .

Athens was conquered in 404. Violent party strife divided the city, and the aristocratic coterie, always pro-Sparta, finally got the upper hand. There was another revolution of the power cycle.

The Spartan Empire lasted only a few years. Toward the end of the war she had made an alliance with her old archenemy, Persia, which helped her greatly in reducing Athens. But soon afterwards the two allies quarrelled. Sparta was defeated and Persia took away the sea empire she had taken away from Athens.

.   .   .

The cause of all these evils was the desire for power which greed and ambition inspire.—*Thucydides* III, 83

PRIVATE IDIOM

I TOLD A DISTINGUISHED young poet, who had lately won a notable prize, that the only line of strictly modern poetry I knew by heart was, "We are the eyelids of defeated caves." He said, "I know the man who wrote that." "Then," I said hopefully, "you can tell me what it means." He meditated. "No," he said, "I cannot. But when I see him I will ask him."

Keats said, "All great poetry should produce the instantaneous conviction, 'This is true.' "

The cult of the incomprehensible, in music, in painting, and in poetry, is spreading and our loss is immeasurable. Those who are struggling to explore and express for us the new universe within, which is so strange to us, sometimes gifted souls who in other ages would have been our seers and interpreters, do not speak to us in a way we can understand. Often it seems that they do not care to, that they are content to be understood only by themselves. So we are losing in this distracted world the illumination of art given by our own contemporaries, spoken by those who live in the same atmosphere with us, the beauty and the elevation and the interpretation of the mystery which artists in other days were able to express to their contemporaries.

. . .

History shows that when a literature floats away from the solid ground of the common speech to a language peculiar to itself, when it disdains the public stage and seeks only a small private audience, it is nearing its end. As the gap widens between the way people talk and the way people write, what is born is a thing called closet literature, quite properly. If it stays shut up in the closet it perishes for lack of air.

. . .

A private idiom for an artist? It is impossible. The man who uses it is either not an artist or else he is too bewildered by what he has discovered in the still dim realm of self-knowledge to be able to find words for it. Art, all art, is communication; writing is especially so. People do not write to themselves. They write to say things to other people. Of course the artists must explore the strange world within themselves which Freud has opened to us as never before, but they must not stay there. If they find they cannot express what they have seen except by using a language comprehensible only to themselves, if "defeated" seems to them applicable to caves—which also have eyelids—then, if they are wise, they will take warning from the past and stop writing until they have come out from the thickets of themselves and are interested in looking at a cave.

Self-knowledge is perhaps won most easily in solitude. But anyone who wants to write what will endure must leave his attic, come down from his ivory tower, and test his discoveries, his truths, in the only final way, by the universal touchstone of their significance in the outside world.

FREEDOM

TO THE GREEKS OF THAT DAY [fifth century B.C.] their most precious possession, freedom, was the distinguishing mark between East and West. Despotism was the form of rule in the East. Despots, as far as the Greeks knew them— there were none in their part of the world—always acted in the same way, clearing the road to the throne by exterminating the royal family, shedding blood without measure, using any means to forward their ends, and generally successful in increasing enormously for a time the power of the state. They did not enslave the people for they were already slaves, helpless masses at the ruler's disposal. Aristotle spoke for Greece when he said that Asiatics were slaves by nature. "You do not know what freedom is," Herodotus reports a Greek saying to a Persian. "If you did you would fight for it with bare hands if you had no weapons."

. . .

The Athenian citizen had true freedom. There has never been a state more free; there have been few as free. Never was freedom of speech restricted; not in times of utmost peril when an enemy was advancing to the very walls of the city. Even then the blunders and failures of politicians and generals were shown up in the theatre as well as discussed by whoever chose; even then at the opening of the Assembly, the ultimate power made up of every Athenian, the presiding officer asked, "Does any one wish to speak?"

· · ·

There has never been a war fought for purer motives than the war against Persia. Marathon and Salamis are still words that "send a ringing challenge down through the generations." Their victories still seem a miracle as they seemed to the men who won them. The mighty were put down from their seats and those of low degree exalted, and for fifty years and more Persia could do nothing to Greece.

What followed was one of the most triumphant rebirths of the human spirit in all history, when the bitter differences that divide men were far in the background and freedom was in the air—freedom in the great sense, not only equality before the law, but freedom of thought and speech.

· · ·

Herodotus is the historian of the glorious fight for liberty in which the Greeks conquered the overwhelming power of Persia. They won the victory because they were free men defending their freedom against a tyrant and his army of slaves. So Herodotus saw the contest. The watchword was freedom; the stake was the independence or the enslavement of Greece; the issue made it sure that Greeks never would be slaves.

The modern reader cannot accept the proud words without a wondering question. What of the slaves these free Greeks owned? The Persian defeat did not set them free. What real idea of freedom could the conquerors at Marathon and Salamis have had, slaveowners, all of them? . . . Life in Greece as everywhere else was founded on slaves.

. . .

From time immemorial that was the attitude in all the world. There was never anywhere a dreamer so rash or so romantic as to imagine a life without slaves. The loftiest thinkers, idealists, and moralists never had an idea that slavery was evil. In the Old Testament it is accepted without comment exactly as in the records of Egypt and Mesopotamia. Even the prophets of Israel did not utter a word against it, nor, for that matter, did St. Paul. What is strange is not that the Greeks took slavery for granted through hundreds of years, but that finally they began to think about it and question it.

To Euripides the glory belongs of being the first to condemn it. "Slavery," he wrote:

> That thing of evil, by its nature evil,
> Forcing submission from a man to what
> No man should yield to.

He was, as usual, far in advance of his age.

A hundred years ago America had to fight a great war before slavery was abolished.

. . .

The following is from a Radio Address written for the Voice of America Roots of Freedom Series.

Some 2,500 years ago Greece discovered freedom. Before that there was no freedom. There were great civilizations, splendid empires, but no freedom anywhere. Egypt, Babylon, Nineveh, were all tyrannies, one immensely powerful man ruling over helpless masses. In Greece, in Athens, a little city in a little country, there were no helpless masses, and a time came when the Athenians were led by a great man who did not want to be powerful.

The creed of the first free government in the world was liberty for all men who could control themselves and would take responsibility for the state. This was the conception that underlay the lofty reach of Greek genius.

But discovering freedom is not like discovering atomic bombs. It cannot be discovered once for all. If people do not prize it, and work for it, it will depart. Eternal vigilance is its price. Athens changed. It was a change that took place unnoticed though it was of the utmost importance, a spiritual change which penetrated the whole state. It had been the Athenians' pride and joy to give to their city. That they could get material benefits from her never entered their minds. There had to be a complete change of attitude before they could look at the city as an employer who paid her citizens for doing her work. Now instead of men giving to the state, the state was to give to them. What the people wanted was a government which would provide a comfortable life for them; and with this as the foremost object, ideas of freedom and self-reliance and responsibility were obscured to the point of disappearing. Athens was more and more looked on as a co-operative business possessed of great wealth in which all citizens had a right to share.

She reached the point when the freedom she really wanted was freedom from responsibility. There could be only one result. If men insisted on being free from the burden of self-dependence and responsibility for the common good, they would cease to be free. Responsibility is the price every man must pay for freedom. It is to be had on no other terms. Athens, the Athens of Ancient Greece, refused responsibility; she reached the end of freedom and was never to have it again.

But, "the excellent becomes the permanent," Aristotle said. Athens lost freedom forever, but freedom was not lost forever for the world. A great American statesman, James Madison, in or near the year 1776 A.D., referred to: "The capacity of mankind for self-government." No doubt he had not an idea that he was speaking Greek. Athens was not in the farthest background of his mind, but once a great and good idea has dawned upon man, it is never completely lost. The Atomic Age cannot destroy it. Somehow in this or that man's thought such an idea lives though unconsidered by the world of action. One can never be sure that it is not on the point of breaking out into action, only sure that it will do so sometime.

. . .

Ideals have enormous power. They stamp an age. They lift life up when they are lofty; they drag down and make decadent when they are low—and then, by that strange fact, the survival of the fittest, those that are low fade away and are forgotten. The Greek ideals have had a power of persistent life for twenty-five hundred years.

. . .

Great men are judged by the heights they reach. Only a poet's best counts; his bad makes no difference at all. We never think of the poor lines Shakespeare could write, of the terrible verses Wordsworth perpetrated. None of that matters. People who achieve greatness anywhere in anything, are remembered for that. The rest of them is dropped out of sight.

. . .

This Address to the Athenians was delivered by Miss Hamilton in the Theatre of Herodes Atticus at the foot of the Acropolis in 1957 on the occasion of her being made a citizen of Athens.

It is impossible for me to express my gratitude for the honors shown me. I am a citizen of Athens, of the city I have for so long loved as much as I love my own country. This is the proudest moment of my life. And yet as I stand here speaking to you under the very shadow of the Acropolis a deeper feeling rises. I see Athens, the home of beauty and of thought. Even today among buildings, the Parthenon is supreme; Plato's thought has never been transcended; of the four great tragedians, three are Greek. We are here to see a performance of the *Prometheus*. In all literature, Prometheus is the great rebel against tyranny. It is most fitting that he should be presented to the world now, in this period of the world's history, and here, in the city of Athens. For Athens, truly the mother of beauty and of thought, is also the mother of freedom. Freedom was a Greek discovery. The Greeks were the first free nation in the world. In the *Prometheus* they have sent a ringing call down through the centuries to all who would be free. Prometheus, confronted with the utmost tyranny, will not submit. He tells the tyrant's messenger, who urges him to yield, "Go and persuade the sea-wave not to break. You will persuade me no more easily." That is the spirit Greece gave to the world. It challenges us and we need the challenge. Greece rose to the very height not because she was big, she was very small; not because she was rich, she was very poor; not even because she was wonderfully gifted. She rose because there was in the Greeks the greatest spirit that moves in humanity, the spirit that makes men free. It is impossible for us to believe that of all the nations of the world, Greece was the only one that had the vision of what St. John in the Gospels calls "the true light," which he adds, "lighteth every man who cometh into the world"; but we know that she was the only one who followed it. She kept on—on what one of her poets calls "the long and rough and steep road." Therefore her light was never extinguished. Therefore we are met tonight to see a play which has lived for 2,500 years. In those years the Greeks have been outstripped by science and technology, but never in the love of the truth, never in the creation of beauty and of freedom.

SOURCES OF
THE SELECTIONS

Following are the works from which the Edith Hamilton excerpts have been selected; page numbers refer to this volume.

PAGES

123   *The Ever-Present Past*, "These Sad Young Men." First
appeared in *The Atlantic Monthly*, May 1929.
Copyright 1929 by The Atlantic Monthly Company. Reprinted by permission.

124   *The Echo of Greece*, Chapter 2, "Athens' Failure."

124–128   *The Greek Way*, Chapter 9, "Thucydides, The Thing
That Hath Been is That Which Shall Be."

129–131   *The Ever-Present Past*, "Private Idiom." First appeared in *Vogue*, September 15, 1951. Copyright
1951, The Condé Nast Publications Inc. Reprinted by permission.

133–134   *The Echo of Greece*, Chapter 1, "Freedom."

134–136   *The Greek Way*, Chapter 9, "Thucydides, The Thing
That Hath Been is That Which Shall Be."

136–138   *The Ever-Present Past*, "Roots of Freedom." A radio
address written for the Voice of America Roots
of Freedom Series, this first appeared in *Greek
Heritage*, Vol. 1, No. 1, Winter 1963. Copyright
© 1963 by the Athenian Corporation.

138   *The Ever-Present Past*, "The Ever-Present Past," and
Witness to the Truth, Chapter 7, "St. Paul."

138–140   *The Ever-Present Past*, "Address to the Athenians."
First appeared under the title "The True Light"
in *Saturday Review*, October 19, 1957.

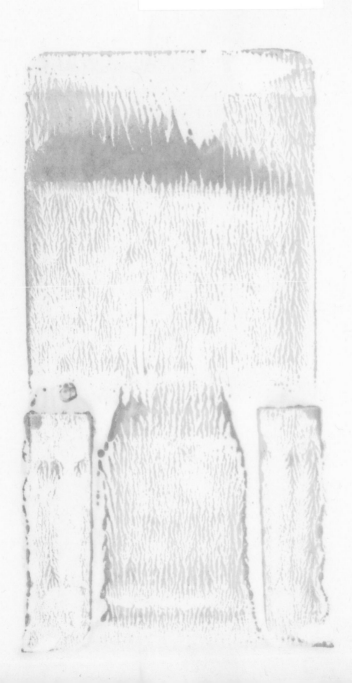